THE HIGH 5 GUIDE

Adventure
Learning Center

CHALLENGE COURSE
OPERATING PROCEDURES
FOR THE THINKING
PRACTITIONER

JIM GROUT
NICKI HALL

Important: The practices, procedures and forms presented in this publication are intended to be used, if at all, as guidelines and examples only. Programs vary greatly, including with respect to goals, clients, staff, environments and activities. A program which uses any part of the material furnished in this publication does so at its own risk. Neither High 5 nor any of its staff, directors or owners is responsible for any outcome of such use.

KENDALL/HUNT   PUBLISHING   COMPANY
4050 Westmark Drive   Dubuque, Iowa 52002

Cover design created by High 5 Adventure.

CONTENTS

ACKNOWLEDGMENTS

The High 5 Guide has been a work in progress for several years. Over time, many people have contributed their ideas and support for this project. We would like to acknowledge the generosity of this help that has finally brought this book to fruition.

First and foremost, the expertise of the High 5 staff has helped to shape this book in numerous ways: Todd Brown with his vast technical knowledge, Melissa Fitzgerald with her willingness to perform all kinds of miracles on the computer and to research photos, Chris Ortiz with his help reviewing the text and offering valuable suggestions, Jennifer Ottinger with her marketing wisdom and artful selection of words and phrases, Jennifer Stanchfield for reviewing the text, generously writing the piece on reflection and contributing photos and Kelly McMillan for pressing us on the need for such a document as it related to our work within High 5's challenge course building department.

Thanks also to Jeff Baird, our professional photographer who, always with good humor and a smile, has taken so many of the photos in this book.

Sandy Kohn, Venture Director at the University of North Carolina Charlotte served as an outside reviewer and his critical eye contributed many important changes and edits to the final version. His efforts are very much appreciated.

It is important to note that this book is really a compilation of facts, information and practices gained from years in the challenge course field. A case in point is the Low and High Challenge Course Operational Guidelines. As industry standards and technology have evolved, so have the LOPs, perhaps beginning with Project Adventure's first published guidelines through various iterations to our document today.

Similarly, our thoughts, our style, our knowledge, our appreciation of adventure have all been influenced by a variety of people along the way. Although it would be impossible to trace each lesson learned, a few deserve mention. They are Karl Rohnke, Bob Ryan, Steve Butler, Charlie Harrington, Cindi Simpson, Chuck Bolesh, Ken Demas and Amy Kohut.

In addition there are numerous colleagues from the Association for Challenge Course Technology ACCT community whose insights and sharing of information have enriched our work over the years.

Thanks to Christine Takacs from Signaltree Marketing & Advertising in Keene, NH. Christine succeeded in presenting rather mundane information in a manner that is both entertaining and easy to read.

As with any project like this, much of it is done at home on nights and weekends, and family support is crucial. Thanks to Colleen, Corey and Nick Grout and Sam Slater for their patience and support throughout.

FOREWORD

I have been fortunate to know Nicki Hall and Jim Grout as friends and colleagues for the past thirty years, since the very infancy of adventure education programs and the challenge course industry. We have together witnessed and been a part of this wonderful educational movement that has grown from a small regional concept to include thousands of challenge courses and tens of thousands of practitioners around the world.

Jim and Nicki are more than qualified to write about the technical skills and managerial knowledge associated with challenge courses. They were part of the group of pioneers of this industry. As founders and veteran staff of High 5 Adventure Learning Center they are at the forefront of professional development within the field and national standards for challenge course technology.

Their unique ability to balance common sense and practicality with increasingly demanding industry standards makes them especially suited to put their wisdom into one comprehensive reference guide for the challenge course practitioner. This book conveys the idea that it is not just technical skills and experience that make top-notch facilitators, but one's ability to develop sound judgment and a critical eye. They call the person who achieves this balance a *thinking practitioner* and have spent the past eight years at High 5 developing training workshops that reflect this concept.

Whether you are new to the field or a veteran, I know that you will find this book an essential reference tool for your continued development as a professional in the field.

Yours in Adventure,

Charlie Harrington
EDGE Director, A Program of the Maine Seacoast Mission

PREFACE

As we write this book, the challenge course industry is in the midst of some of the most significant changes in its three-decade plus history. Practitioner certification guidelines and governmental regulation are changing the way we do business more than ever before. Whether or not we agree with these changes matters little, for change is inevitable. We all must now determine how to best adapt to these changes.

It is a given that we must use our technical skills to deliver challenge course experiences within a safe environment. But in this era of growing requirements and regulations from many directions, administrators, insurance companies, government regulators and our industry itself, it is important not to let all of this *become* the program. Over our 28 years in the field of adventure we have always thought that experiential education can be defined simply: it is an educational tool for helping people develop as a person. When we have found ourselves challenged with what feels like too much information and regulation, too many details and choices, we go back to that simple definition for perspective.

Most skills-based training workshops contain an enormous amount of information to absorb. It can feel overwhelming at times for participants to remember how to tie the right knot, choose an appropriate game or initiative, facilitate a debrief, set up a belay or put on a harness properly. Program managers are also taxed with the additional responsibilities of training and managing staff, developing local operating procedures and staying current with trends in the field.

It is because of all this that I (Jim) end my training workshops by telling participants, "When in doubt, give them your heart." It reminds people that the essence of what we do as adventure educators is to *provide people with a powerful learning experience that is engaging, challenging, thought provoking and fun.*

We hope that this book will serve as a resource to help readers achieve the magical balance between technical skills and thoughtful facilitation, to create the best and most powerful experience for your audience.

So by all means dot the I's, cross the T's, learn your skills and learn them well. But then make sure to connect and inspire those with whom you work.

Jim Grout & Nicki Hall

INTRODUCTION

Intentional Programming

Why Does Your Program Do What It Does? This may seem like an odd question with which to begin a manual about the operation of challenge course elements. You might think that the most relevant information for guiding one's actions would immediately address issues such as spotting, knot tying and belaying.

While it is true that these are critical skills for the adventure practitioner to have mastered, of equal importance is an understanding of one's program: its purpose, goals and desired outcomes.

A program's mission and vision shape the program design in such a way that decision making regarding the necessary equipment (from game bags to challenge course elements), staffing needs and training requirements becomes self evident. Knowing how to utilize the various elements on a challenge course is but one piece of the puzzle that constitutes thoughtful and purposeful programming.

Thinking Practitioners

At High 5, we pride ourselves on creating "thinking practitioners" who, in turn, create "thoughtful programs." As a non-profit educational organization, this approach is an integral part of our High 5 mission and regularly guides our program designs, organizational decisions and the type of work we pursue and develop. And, as you will see in the following pages, it even guides the way in which this manual is structured. Before you get to the pages dealing with the nuts and bolts of proper operating procedures and risk management, you will encounter our thoughts about mission, program design, sequencing and reflection. Our purpose in doing this is to emphasize the integral connection between thoughtful programming conducted by skilled practitioners and the degree to which programs effectively institute proper procedures and manage risks.

With that said, you will in fact find that a great portion of this manual is devoted to outlining proper operating procedures for challenge course activities. These procedures have been developed and refined over many years and are a reflection of current High 5 practices, those of other vendors in the field and the standards established by the Association for Challenge Course Technology (ACCT).

It is worth noting that operating procedures can vary significantly. Some common questions that reflect this truth are:

- **How broad is the range of acceptable practices within the field?**

- **Do different operating systems require different skill sets?**

- **How does one determine when a practice is "unsafe," as opposed to "unfamiliar"?**

- **What constitutes a "mainstream" practice?**

- **Can a local operating procedure[1] differ from a mainstream practice?**

These questions, and many more like them, require us to categorize our thinking. Over the years, we have consistently instructed practitioners in our training workshops to avoid having a practice or procedure at their site that does not exist anywhere else.

While this may be a tribute to their creative ingenuity, it is a good idea to keep one's local operating procedures (LOP) as a reflection of the common practices in the field (often referred to as standard operating procedures). You can always do more than what is expected by mainstream practices but should avoid doing less.

For example, some years ago, helmets were not always worn on every high element. Rather, this practice was limited to those elements on which one could bump her head, i.e., Dangle Duo, Cat Walk, etc. Such a practice written into one's LOP was very acceptable as it followed mainstream practices. However, over time, the norm became that helmets were worn by all participants on all high elements. If one's LOP continued to reflect the old practice of specified use according to the element, it would have been out of synch with what had now become a mainstream practice.

This manual outlines operating procedures that are commonplace within the challenge course industry and would be considered generally acceptable practices. It does not attempt to address practices that may be specific to a particular operating system.

---

1 Local Operating Procedures are defined as those policies and procedures for operating all facets of one's program, including site-specific information on various challenge course elements.

In addition to there being many ways to do things, it is important to realize that standards can also change over time. In the thirty-plus years that challenge courses have been part of the adventure education industry, practices have changed and evolved. This evolution has occurred for several different reasons. Some that existed years ago are still sound practices today. Others have been altered for a variety of reasons including: refinements in equipment or technology, the maturation of adventure education philosophies, the review of the causes of past accidents and an increased understanding of how individuals learn and grow. It is the job of the adventure practitioner to stay current with trends and changes in the field and to make sure that one's local operating procedures accurately reflect those changes. As a leading training organization in the field, we certainly see one of our responsibilities to be to help you achieve this goal. This manual and the accompanying LOP-CD template is our attempt to do just that.

It is our hope that you will find this manual to be "user friendly." It is written as a guide (thus the title, *The High 5 Guide*) for both the novice and the veteran practitioner. It is not intended to take the place of proper training. Books, CD's, DVD's and other supplemental materials are just that, supplemental, and should never be considered as a substitute for hands-on training.

Having conducted skills training workshops for thousands of adventure practitioners, we believe it is simply a "best practice" to attend professional workshops on a regular basis as part of one's adventure learning path. A good learning environment, with a healthy exchange of ideas and experiences, helps create "thinking practitioners" who can think on their feet and respond appropriately to challenging leadership situations.

A WORD ON USING THIS GUIDE

It is our hope that this Introduction has begun to set the tone for accomplishing our two goals for this book: 1) that you gain an understanding and appreciation for the importance of having whatever you do be driven by your program philosophy, and 2) that it provides you with sound information regarding standard operating procedures for low and high challenge course activities and elements.

SECTION 1 will focus upon the role that mission and philosophy play in shaping your program. We will spend some time examining High 5 as an organization and how decisions we have made have shaped who we are and how we approach our role as an adventure education organization.

SECTION 2 will take a look at the particulars of managing an adventure program and the multitude of topics that such a charge encompasses.

SECTION 3 will share some ideas on program design, sequencing and facilitation tips and their relationship to sound programming and risk management.

SECTION 4 covers the operating procedures for low and high challenge course elements. The elements included are ones that are common within the field and that we typically build as part of High 5's challenge course installation services. Indoor elements appear in a separate section after low and high outdoor elements.

SECTION 5 has various forms mentioned throughout the text, an Appendix, a Bibliography and our collective thoughts on the various "Thinking Practitioner" questions posed throughout the book. These questions are intended to cause you to ponder and reflect about a variety of practices, situations and beliefs frequently encountered by practitioners. Our thoughts are simply our "best" thoughts on the subject but may be slightly skewed to a High 5 way of thinking. Feel free to add your own opinion and even give us a call to share, debate or expand thoughts on the various subjects.

Happy reading and "thinking"!

Jim Grout & Nicki Hall

MISSION & PHILOSOPHY

CAUGHT YOU THINKING #1:

Our school just got

$12,000 to build a

climbing wall,

can you help us?

MISSION & PHILOSOPHY

SO...WHY DOES YOUR PROGRAM DO WHAT IT DOES?

This seems like a simple question right? We touched on this question in the introduction, but now we will look at it a bit more in depth.

All too often as programs develop over time and staff members come and go, the purpose, direction and intent of a program become less clear. For example, a youth service agency builds a challenge course and trains its staff to develop an adventure program for the youth served by the agency. In an effort to recover some of the costs invested in the challenge course, a decision is made to solicit outside groups from the community, particularly corporate groups, to use the course for teambuilding days. Over time, the number of outside groups utilizing the course and its staff outnumbers the programs that are being provided for their young people. The original intent of developing the program has been compromised and the staff has become less clear what their priorities should be, internal programs for kids or money-making programs for external groups.

While this is a very obvious example of "mission lost," albeit a true case, there are countless other examples of programs that start in one direction and slowly end up in another. Frequently this occurs because programs attempt to go in too many directions at once or, in the pursuit of income, lose sight of whom they are trying to serve and what their original intent was.

The remedy for such a dilemma goes back to answering the question, Why Does Your Program Do What It Does? Taking the time to define the mission of your program is an exercise that can help capture the essence of your program philosophy. Whether you are a high school adventure program, a youth service agency or a private vendor of adventure programs, knowing what you are all about and what you do best and then doing it very well, is the key to running a successful and quality program.

When we started High 5 some years ago, we took a long hard look at what we wanted High 5 to become. We defined a direction and said yes to some things and no to others. As a staff we re-visit our mission and direction regularly and thoughtfully make changes as needed.

When you are clear about the purpose of your program, it becomes much easier to make appropriate decisions about things such as the budget, building a challenge course (or not), what equipment to purchase and what type of training you and your staff need.

Let us take a look at our High 5 mission as a means of analyzing what it is telling us about the programs we offer and the decisions and choices we make as an organization.

DETERMINING YOUR MISSION

High 5 Adventure Learning Center is a non-profit educational organization dedicated to helping individuals, schools and communities use experiential education as a tool for improving the way they live, learn and work together.

High 5 is a source of quality, affordable training for all age groups, develops and installs challenge courses and is an educational resource for practitioners in the adventure field who are seeking to expand their knowledge.

We strive to promote adventure experiences that:

- **Develop a sense of community**
- **Present both physical and emotional challenge**
- **Improve program and technical competence**
- **Are fun and enjoyable**
- **Provide an environment of learning and discovery**
- **Empower people, build programs and create vision**

So what does this mean for High 5 as an organization? How does it provide direction and help determine its programs?

Too often mission language is just that, language. To illustrate how High 5 uses its mission and philosophy to actively shape its decisions, let's use a familiar activity most associated with helping a group develop their behavior norms called Quick Norms or US/NOT US. In this case the "group" is High 5, the organization.

When this is used with a group, the directions are simply to ask the participants to create two columns on a piece of newsprint: one that represents the US and the other that represents NOT US. The US column gets filled with words that describe the behavior of the group that is desired, i.e., communicative, caring, safety conscious, fun, etc. The other column is filled with words that the group does not want to have as part of their behaviors, i.e. sarcasm, put downs, not listening, not valuing all opinions, etc.

In this instance, the goal is to create US and NOT US columns based upon the mission and philosophy of High 5.

HIGH 5 ADVENTURE LEARNING CENTER ORGANIZATIONAL BEHAVIOR NORMS BASED UPON OUR MISSION AND PHILOSOPHY

US	NOT US
• educational org./non-profit	• doing too much corporate work
• being affordable	• being overpriced
• being an educational resource/sharing	• being overprotective of materials
• being program driven	• product-driven sales
• maintaining program focus	• trying to do too many things
• developing a strong staff community	• having high staff turnover
• having a highly experienced staff	• lacking experience
• saying "no" to jobs that do not fit our mission	• accepting any kind of work
• readily sharing our work & ideas within the field	• not growing/staying insular
• having long-term customers	• short programs that lack connection
• being friendly and available	• not being available to customers
• promoting healthy challenge/being experiential	• forgetting our exp. educational roots
• creating an exciting learning environment	• being too didactic in our approach

While this norm chart may look simple, it can be challenging to stay true to the desired behaviors on a day-to-day basis. But, like a compass, if we refer to it regularly it can remind us when we have veered off course. Just as no group is able to realize their ideal behavior every moment of a workshop, no organization can maintain its desired direction without periodically getting lost. Asking ourselves, "Why our program does what it does," serves us well and initiates some corrective action when we need it.

So what does all this mean for you, your organization and its programs?

We recommend that you do your homework. Take the time to create and reflect about the work your organization does and then make some decisions regarding what needs to continue and what needs to change.

A quick way to determine if your program needs to further define its direction is to look for the following telltale signs.

- **There is lack of clarity among staff regarding the question, "Why does your program do what it does?"**
- **Programming appears to be lacking purpose and sequence***
- **Staff skill sets do not match program needs***
- **Programming is all about the challenge course**
- **Reflection time with participants is minimal**
- **Incidents/accidents are occurring too regularly***
- **Staff turnover is high***
- **There is no established training plan for staff***
- **The program has no designated manager/coordinator***

If you recall, part of the purpose of this chapter is to illustrate the importance of having thoughtful programs drive your organization. There is also a strong case for the connection between thoughtful programming and safety and risk management. Note the starred items in the list above. Each of them is related to issues of risk management.

Statistically, the number one cause of incidents and accidents on challenge courses is under-trained staff. Many of the above indicators are connected to this issue. Thinking practitioners create thoughtful programs that manage risks effectively.

For example: We were asked to do a program evaluation at a site that was experiencing an unusual number of scrapes and bruises from one of their low elements, the Mohawk Walk.

CAUGHT YOU THINKING #2:

My director

just asked me to

increase the number

of people I can

get through the chal-

lenge course

from 30 to 45

people per hour.

What should I do?

CAUGHT YOU THINKING #3:

Our director hired a marketing consultant to help us increase revenues 15–20% over the next three to five years. He recommended a heavy focus on bringing in corporate programs for teambuilding days.

Staff from the site said that almost every time they used the element, someone received a minor injury. They also said that this had been going on for some time. After the last incident occurred they felt they should confer with someone who does training to see if in fact this was typical. We conducted a site visit to watch a program in action. It became immediately clear that staff was very under-trained in that basic operating procedures for the element were not being followed, i.e., proper spotting, staff-to-student ratios and group behavior expectations for using challenge course activities in general. The obvious remedy here would be simply to have the staff be trained in and/or review proper procedures.

MANAGING AN ADVENTURE PROGRAM

MANAGING AN ADVENTURE PROGRAM

One of the first activities we do in our High 5 workshop, Managing an Adventure Program, is a blindfolded puzzle initiative. While this classic activity is generally used as a teambuilding initiative, in this instance, the focus is less on teambuilding and more on the role of each participant as a program manager. Each puzzle piece is labeled with the various topics that program managers need to be prepared to address. For example: staff development, local operating procedures, risk management, accidents/incidents, medical screening, etc. Participants are instructed to begin to assemble the pieces blindfolded. On occasion, one sighted person is allowed, but may only answer "yes" or "no" to any question asked.

The activity lends itself to some powerful metaphors about the role of program managers, as the puzzle is representative of the many tasks they face in fulfilling that role. Thoughtful managers must be able to identify and prioritize a multitude of topics on a regular basis if their programs are to run effectively. Determining which topics need the most attention at a particular time requires skill and experience. Putting the puzzle of program management together is challenging and it is not unusual for a manager to feel like she is operating in isolation (i.e., blindfolded), lacking guidance or information beyond their own site or program. In the spirit of not operating in the dark, let's take a look at those topics.

START WITH PROGRAM DESIGN

Designing programs to meet the needs of individuals, groups and organizations is a desirable goal. However, program design is not always considered a priority topic when one thinks of program management issues. Frequently the emphasis is placed on the more technical topics such as staff training, equipment readiness, insurance, medical forms etc. In our view it should be viewed as an integral part of the program management scheme. A good program design accomplishes a couple of things. First, it assures that the program you deliver to your participants will more than likely be successful and, secondly, it reduces the risk of engaging participants in something that they are not ready for. Well designed programs are more valuable, more enjoyable and allow facilitators to manage risks more effectively. (Note: For more thoughts on program design see Section 3.)

STAFF DEVELOPMENT & TRAINING

Good people with good training create good programs. Finding and cultivating talented, skilled, friendly people takes effort but there is no more important part of a program than the staff who delivers it. Experienced, well-trained staff, who exercise good judgment, will generally conduct quality programs that manage risks effectively.

How does a program make this happen? It starts with valuing the importance of training. Too often, programs invest the yeoman's share of their budget into equipment, i.e., the challenge course, and consider training as an afterthought. Some points to consider:

Hiring Staff

We used to think hiring was as simple as finding that right person with a certain twinkle in their eye. While such an approach conjures up a good image, it probably constitutes a rather weak hiring plan. With that said, there is a strength in hiring people who project energy, have people skills and create a presence that makes a group want to be with them. These traits, coupled with strong facilitation and technical skills, can make for a good candidate. Matching a person's past experience and current skill set to the needs of your position is crucial. Obviously the person being asked to deliver direct service programs to youth has a different profile than someone expected to lead training workshops for professionals.

It has become easier to find skilled adventure practitioners than it was some years ago. This is attributable to the overall growth of the industry which has included more colleges and universities offering degrees in outdoor education, thus supplying the field with a higher skill level of job applicants.

CAUGHT YOU THINKING #4:

I'd like to bring 35 eighth graders for a day of challenge course activities. We'll arrive at 9 am and need to leave by 2 pm. We'd like to have everybody do at least one high element. Our budget is limited, so I thought perhaps some of our teachers could help belay. Please get back to me as soon as possible.

Qualifications

A recently graduated college student once called High 5 to inquire about which workshop she should enroll in, Adventure Basics, an introductory workshop, or Beyond Basics, an advanced level one. We asked her how much experience she had and she indicated she had had a full semester course during her senior year. When asked if it was "a lot" of hours, she responded, "Oh yes, it must have been at least fifteen." Gulp! Seems that it is all in one's perspective as to what constitutes "a lot." For the purpose of this discussion regarding qualifications, let's agree that fifteen is NOT a lot of hours. And hours aside, the real question is what does it take for someone to be qualified? The next obvious question is, "Qualified for what?" The answer to this depends greatly upon the role the person is being asked to fulfill (i.e., lead instructor, assistant instructor, etc.) and the activities they will be charged with facilitating. For example, a camp staff member responsible only for doing games, initiatives and low elements does not need the same qualifications as the person leading groups on a challenge course with high elements. Standards for facilitators have improved greatly in recent years as the growth of the field has required everyone to be more conscious of what constitutes adequate training. When certification standards are finalized and embraced by the entire industry it will only help to clarify what it means to be qualified. Practitioners will not only have completed a course or training, but will have been able to demonstrate actual competencies.

CAUGHT YOU THINKING #5:

How much training do I need?

How do I know if I know enough?

On-going Training

Like any profession, the skill development of the adventure practitioner should be continuous. Training should begin with a solid foundation of basic skills and be updated regularly to stay current with best practices in the field and with the needs of one's program.

In-House Training versus Professional Training

Probably the best way to think about this issue is to eliminate the word versus because quality training of both types makes good sense. As mentioned previously, the field of adventure education has grown exponentially over the years and the need for high-quality, competency-based training is quite clear. Professional trainings by outside individuals or organizations are a vital piece of every organization's training plan. Additionally, in-house trainings that refresh and re-visit the various skill sets are invaluable to maintaining good practices among staff.

However, it is not a good practice for a program to conduct internal trainings only. Often a staff person who attends a professional training provided by an external vendor may want to come back to train others on her staff. Too often these efforts include only a fraction of the time and content of the original training. They also tend to focus on technical skills only with insufficient time spent on the broader but equally important topics such as program design, proper sequencing, program philosophy, etc. These "second" and "third" generation trainings can result in low quality over time.

A staff development plan that works well would consist of on-going internal and external trainings that measure participant competencies and thoughtfully match staffs' skills with program needs.

PRACTITIONER CERTIFICATION

Several professional training organizations have developed their own in-house "certification" systems. Others give participants a certificate of attendance or a certificate of "successful completion." Ultimately, any training program should focus on the core competencies necessary to facilitate a challenge course program to the level accepted as standard in the field. The Association for Challenge Course Technology, ACCT, established operational standards for the use of challenge courses some years ago. These are available through ACCT (see www.acctinfo.org) and appear in the ACCT Standards Manual. While these operational standards are a helpful guideline for organizations as best practices, they are not to be confused with certification standards. There are currently efforts within the field, via ACCT, to establish a set of practitioner certification standards for the industry. Such a set of standards would provide a common guide for the certification of adventure practitioners in the future. As the field has grown and developed over the years, it has become evident that some common language and interpretation around certification is needed, thus providing a clearer picture as to what competencies have been attained through the training one has received.

HIGH 5 ADVENTURE LEARNING CENTER PRACTITIONER CERTIFICATION PROGRAM

High 5's Practitioner Certification Program is designed to complement our various training programs.

As a Level 4 Professional Vendor Member of the Association for Challenge Course Technology (ACCT), High 5's certification program is required to meet the practitioner certification standards developed by ACCT. As with our trainings, our certification program focuses on the technical skills and core competencies necessary to facilitate a challenge course program to the level accepted as standard in the field. Our certification process is designed to be intensive, professional, thorough and enjoyable.

The High 5 Practitioner Certification process takes place separately from our training workshops. The primary reason for this separation is to preserve an exciting, non-pressured learning environment within our training workshops that accommodates the varied learning pace of participants.

Practitioner Certification Workshops are scheduled specifically for the purpose of verifying technical skills for those desiring certification. These day programs include both written and practical tests and take place both at our High 5 training site and at various locations around the Northeast (United States). They are offered several times a year.

We currently offer three levels of certification for practitioners:

LEVEL 1 Challenge Course Instructor

A Level 1 Practitioner will have received a minimum of 50 hours of training based upon attendance at a High 5 Adventure Basics five-day workshop (or its equivalent) and one other skills-based workshop of 1-2 days in length. Participants must show competency and an understanding of basic program facilitation skills and technical skills. Participants should have a minimum 100 hours of program experience as a facilitator on a challenge course.

Level 1 is designed for practitioners who facilitate lead-up activities and low and high challenge course elements. Testing includes written and practical tests. The written test must be passed with a score of at least 80%. Participants must show mastery of all practical skills. Testing at this level takes place over a one-day period. Level 1 certification must be renewed annually.

LEVEL 2 Challenge Course Instructor

A Level 2 Practitioner will possess an advanced level of program knowledge and advanced competencies in the areas of facilitation and technical skills. Participants will have received a minimum of 85 hours of training (this includes the 50 hours from Level 1) based upon attendance at a High 5's Beyond Basics four-day workshop (or its equivalent). Participants should have a minimum 200 hours of program experience as a facilitator on a challenge course. This experience should include high elements.

Level 2 is designed for practitioners who facilitate all low and high challenge course elements. Testing includes specialty skill areas such as challenge course rescues and a written and practical test. The written test must be passed with a score of at least 80%. Participants must show mastery of all practical skills. Testing at this level takes place over a one-day period. Level 2 certification must be renewed every three years.

LEVEL 3 Challenge Course Manager

The Challenge Course Manager certification requires a minimum of 30 hours of training in topics specific to program management. High 5's three-day Managing an Adventure Program workshop (or its equivalent) meets this requirement. Participants must also have completed Level 2 certification and have a minimum 500 hours of program experience. This certification is designed for those individuals responsible for program management at their site, i.e., program directors, challenge course coordinators.

Testing at this level includes a written exam only and is conducted in a half-day workshop format.

Note: Not all programs need a certified challenge course manager. Depending upon the size and scope of one's program, these responsibilities may be incorporated to the degree necessary within the Level 2 certification.

High 5's Practitioner Certification Program is designed to help adventure practitioners achieve and maintain a high level of facilitation skill and technical competence.

A combination of training workshops and/or certification is the best route to assuring that practitioners develop and maintain the necessary skills to acquire and maintain competency.

Interested candidates for certification should discuss their needs with a certifying vendor to determine the appropriate steps.

NOTE:

- *At publication time, practioner certification standards have been approved by the Association for Challenge Course Technology and will be published in 2007.*

- *In some instances, the hourly requirements for various certification levels exceed ACCT standards as they are currently written. The explanation for this is simply that we at High 5 feel the need to emphasize the importance of hours of experience prior to a person attempting to become certified. Our numbers reflect our thinking on this issue.*

- *High 5's certification process may change as ACCT practitioner standards are refined and implemented over the next several years.*

In an ongoing effort to educate our High 5 clients about program management issues, we typically send the following letter prior to the start of the program season. It includes some thoughtful questions along with recommendations for identifying staff training needs and basic program management tips.

Sample Letter:

Dear Adventure Program Manager,

Here's hoping you've had a good winter and are successfully gearing up for the new adventure season. Here at High 5 we are getting ready as well, which is our purpose in writing you.

The need for programs to have a clear understanding of the challenges and complexities involved in running safe and successful challenge course programs has always been a major task. Recent developments in the field such as practitioner certification and various state regulations have also added to those challenges. Programs vary greatly in both their understanding and capabilities regarding what is needed to run a quality adventure education/challenge course program. The intent of this letter is to clarify some of the key issues and give you a tool to better assess your program's situation and to make any appropriate changes.

Outlined below are some recommendations for practices and procedures to strengthen your program and manage risks more effectively. It is our hope that this will guide you in your preparation plans for the upcoming season. It will also help frame the discussion when you call us regarding the training of staff.

While this list of recommendations may seem a bit overwhelming, it is reflective of the realities that exist within the adventure field today. Every program wants maximum safety at minimum costs and hassle. Unfortunately, these two goals are somewhat mutually exclusive. The key to working successfully with this reality is to carefully match the design of your adventure education program with the time and financial resources that you can honestly devote to it.

Thank you for taking the time to read this letter and give us a call if you have any questions.

Sincerely,

Your friends at High 5

Letter from p. 15 continued

Recommended Practices and Procedures to Strengthen Programs and Manage Risks Effectively

PROGRAM QUESTIONS:

- **What goal(s) are you trying to achieve by having your students/ campers/clients participate in adventure education activities?**

- **What role does the challenge course play in helping achieve those goals?**

Based upon your answer to the questions above, determine what your program will include as part of its curriculum.

For example:

- Games & Initiatives only

- Games, Initiatives, Trust activities & Low Challenge Elements

- Games, Initiatives, Trust activities & Low and High Challenge Elements

STAFF TRAINING:

Match the necessary staff training to the level of program you have.

For example:

- Games & Initiatives =
  1-2 days of training (16-20 hours)

- Games & Initiatives, Trust Activities & Low Challenge Elements =
  2-3 days of training with a skills follow-up on an annual basis
  (24-30 hours)*

- Games, Initiatives, Lows & Highs =
  4-5 days of training with a skills follow-up on an annual basis
  (40-50 hours)*

NOTE: We strongly urge sites with high elements only to consider ways to broaden their program to include a sequence of activities that helps participants adequately prepare for the high elements.

Training hours are approximations based upon High 5 workshop timeframes and other vendors in the field. They also parallel practitioner certification standards developed by vendors of ACCT.

Trainings that involve technical skills for low and high elements should be immersion trainings when possible, i.e. consecutive days.

PROGRAM MANAGEMENT ISSUES:

- If you have a challenge course as part of your program, designate a manager to coordinate the site and the other staff who are assisting with the program. Adequately train the manager both in the appropriate technical skills and in those skills necessary for challenge course management. i.e., Adventure Basics, Beyond Basics, Managing an Adventure Program or their equivalents.

- Train only a limited number of other staff to work as part of the adventure program and train them adequately based upon what they will be expected to deliver. In general, it is a good practice to avoid training someone in one isolated technical skill; i.e., as a belayer, running the Zip Wire, etc. (Note: There may be site-specific reasons when such limited training is necessary but it is recommended that it not be the norm.)

- Do not expect an internal person with limited training to be able to provide the necessary training for the rest of the staff in all skill areas. While it is relatively easy for someone to train other staff in Games and Initiatives, it is not always wise to have that person conduct the technical skill training needed for the safe operation of Low and High Challenge Course elements.

- If you do provide any internal training, it should be conducted by a staff member that has had adequate, professional training. The internal training should reflect the time equivalents outlined above, as these reflect typical norms within the challenge course industry.

- Assure that your program has a set of local operating procedures and that all staff are well versed in them.

- Assure that your challenge course is inspected annually according to ACCT standards

SAFETY, RISK MANAGEMENT & LIABILITY

Safety, risk management and liability are three terms that when used together in a sentence cause undo anxiety to the average adventure practitioner. The word safety is not too bad in and of itself. We basically understand its meaning and can generally agree that safety is a good thing and should be a common goal for all programs. Risk management is another thing all together. It is such an all-inclusive term with so many facets that one can easily feel overwhelmed with the multitude of responsibilities that the term conjures up. And then there is liability; and the one thing that most people will agree upon about liability is that they do not want any!

However, promoting safety, managing risks and understanding liability are tasks that are quite doable when one understands the basic concepts of each.

Promoting safety does not mean that risk of injury has been eliminated. Adventure programs, like any other programs, have risks—both perceived and real. Fortunately the perceived risks outweigh the actual risks. Injury data over the years have consistently shown that adventure education programs have fewer injuries than some team sports and many other physical activities. This successful track record has developed over the years because many programs have done a laudable job of emphasizing the importance of safety and thoughtfully managing the risks associated with participation.

Managing risks involves tending to topics such as program assessment and design, staff development and training, course and equipment inspection and policies and procedures.

Challenge Course Inspection & Equipment Tips

ANNUAL INSPECTION

According to ACCT standards, an annual inspection of a challenge course is required. It should be conducted by a qualified challenge course professional and should include a written inspection report. The ACCT web site is a good resource for qualified vendors that are in your region, **www.acctinfo.org**.

We recommend that you select a course inspector that you have confidence in and that is familiar with your type of course. We also suggest that you maintain that relationship. We frequently are asked if sites should change vendors to get another opinion of their course. While this certainly makes sense if you are not pleased with your current vendor, simply changing vendors for this purpose alone or to save a little money is unwise. A vendor that knows your course and your program will be able to help you with issues such as analyzing any problems on your course, adding appropriate new elements and keeping you current with any developments in the field that may affect your program. Keeping the same vendor can also help with consistency issues around the interpretation of ACCT standards. While most inspectors make every effort to interpret these standards in a similar manner, there are vendor preferences that are stylistic and changing vendors can cause some confusion when two or three different companies get involved with your challenge course.

SEASONAL & DAILY INSPECTION

In addition to the annual inspection, programs should conduct their own inspections on a regular basis. In this instance regular means two things, seasonal and daily.

Seasonal inspections or those done as conditions may dictate due to weather (on outdoor courses), high volume of use, etc. should be assigned to your course manager or some staff person who is familiar with the course construction. Many things can occur that can alter the condition of the course between annual inspection dates. Other daily inspections are the responsibility of all staff utilizing the course.

It is recommended that you have a means for communicating any problems with the course to all staff whether they are in-house full-time people or adjunct staff who use the course occasionally. At High 5 we use emails and a white board posted in our equipment shed. Issues and concerns can be readily posted for the next facilitator to see before the next program begins.

CAUGHT YOU THINKING #6:

A GriGri belay device makes belaying safer.

Some things to look for on a seasonal or daily basis can include the following:

OVERHANGING LIMBS AND EYE LEVEL LIMBS

Any loose, dead limbs that overhang an area where participants will be congregating or passing are a hazard. Small limbs, (particularly on white pine where they often shatter and cause jagged ends) that extend from the trunk on the lower seven feet are potential body (eye) puncturing hazards. Cut all such limbs flush with the trunk.

VANDALISM

On occasion, challenge course elements have fallen prey to vandalism. Daily set-up should include an inspection for any signs that someone has tampered with the course, i.e., moved equipment, downed haul cords, etc.

INSECTS & SMALL ANIMALS

Nests of hornets, bees and wasps can create havoc for the unsuspecting programmer and her participants. Removing nests from climbing towers and other elements that sometimes harbor them can prevent possible medical problems. Outdoor sheds are vulnerable to creatures that live in the area, i.e., mice or squirrels. They like to build nests in cozy areas of the equipment and/or certain elements and can even chew on ropes and harnesses. Climbing ropes stored in nylon or mesh bags are particularly appealing locations for nesting. Look for signs of unwanted visitors and deal with them accordingly. Such damage would only be detected by the critical eye of the facilitator conducting the days' program

WEATHER DAMAGE

On occasion severe weather can cause damage to challenge course elements. Weather hazards can range from lightening strikes to strong winds. Inspection after such storms should be a regular practice.

Trees struck by lightening may indicate damage to cables whether or not the tree has an element attached. Lightening can oftentimes strike a cable and then jump to a nearby tree. Inspection should include a close examination of any cables in the vicinity of a strike. It is recommended that a professional inspection be done if there is any doubt as to storm damage.

METAL-TO-METAL WEAR

Any place where there is metal-to-metal contact with some associated movement, be it carabiner on cable, strandvise bail on nut eye bolt or thimble on quick link, there is the possibility and eventuality of wear. A visual inspection should always look for this type of wear and monitor it carefully.

CAUGHT YOU THINKING #7:

What is a

Nut Eye Bolt?

Do I need to know?

CABLE CLAMPS

We recommend doing a periodic visual inspection of cable clamps to check tightness. Cable clamps should be very tight, tighter than you can achieve by hand. Loose cable clamps should be tightened using a regulation 1/2" drive with a 3/4" socket. Tighten the two nuts by degrees, and torque back and forth from nut to nut during the tightening sequence. Tighten until the clamp looks like it is crimping the cable.

FRAYED CABLE ENDS

Sounds like a cosmetic concern, but protruding wire strands of a frayed cable are a hazard that requires a quick tending to. Check to see that each loose cable working-end is secured by a serving sleeve or (on a temporary basis) by heavy duty tape.

TIGHTNESS OF HARDWARE

Check all nuts that secure the nut eye bolts or threaded eye bolts on support trees or poles. You will seldom find a loose nut on a through-bolt placed in a tree because of the tree's annual increase in girth. Through bolts in utility poles, particularly in geographic areas that have hot, dry climates, will characteristically loosen. An additional spring (lock) washer is included in the tightening package to alleviate this problem. As with bolts, staples in trees generally do not loosen. However the security of staples placed in utility poles can be affected as poles dry and shrink.

EXTREME WEAR DUE TO HIGH VOLUME OF USE

This is not a common problem, in fact it is quite rare, but annual inspections sometimes reveal significant wear to elements that have received high volumes of use. We recommend having staff pay extra attention to the inspection of equipment in areas of high use.

GROUND COVER

Without a covering of wood chips or some other type of organic mulch, a high volume of foot traffic on a challenge course will cause soil compaction. This causes the ground to become hard-packed and roots will begin to show above the surface. Water then cannot make its way to the tree roots. Over a period of time, the affected trees will wither, weaken and die. To prevent this, we recommend spreading six inches of organic material (not treated wood chips) over all areas of consistent foot traffic. Because of ongoing decomposition, this should be done annually.

Equipment Storage and Recordkeeping:

STORAGE

An organized and neat equipment shed or storage room instills confidence in workshop participants and implies that other facets of the program are being managed thoughtfully. Avoid using storage areas where materials that are toxic to ropes and harnesses could be kept (like gasoline, paints, etc.).

ROPE LOGS

There has been much discussion over the years about the best method for keeping track of rope usage. Various systems have included hours of use and the number of climbs. It is recommended that some form of record keeping be done as it shows conscientious management practices (similar to the way an organized equipment shed does). Logs may include the date a rope was put into use and its history of use, i.e., number of climbs or hours of use. However, such record keeping does not accurately dictate the retirement date of one's ropes. The most accurate measure of this is a regular visual and tactile inspection with every use. Specific manufacturers' recommendations for rope retirement should also be known.

INVENTORY

An annual inspection report should include a review of the entire inventory of all equipment on the course. It is recommended that you also have a record of when equipment was purchased and put into use. Conducting an annual inventory of equipment is a convenient time to gather all the equipment in one place, inspect it for wear, assure that it is in good working order and even clean items that are soiled. At High 5 we typically do this kind of thing in winter during our slow season. Such a practice inevitably raises the question of whether to leave belay hardware (pulley, shear reduction device) up on an element all year. We generally recommend that programs take all the gear down once a year for a couple of reasons. While weather, even winter weather, can do little to damage the hardware, it is a good practice to visually inspect the belay hardware in addition to what takes place during the annual inspection. Rapid links that connect the pulley to the shear-reduction device will become very difficult to remove if they remain closed year after year. We typically add a bit of grease to the threads during our seasonal removal practice and this assures that the gates open and close readily. We also clean any sap (from white pine trees) that has accumulated on the hardware over the course of the season.

In addition to getting an opportunity to handle and inspect the belay gear, removing hardware gives staff an opportunity to practice their climbing, gear set-up and gear-retrieval skills. Whether your course is in northern Maine or southern Texas, it is always a good idea to know what is up there and periodically take it down to give it a critical eye.

Local Operating Procedures

Some years ago, we began including a sample of our High 5 local operating procedures in CD form with our training workshops. We did this for the simple reason that too many programs were operating without one. We wanted to encourage workshop participants upon completion of their training to return to their site and revise our sample into an LOP. This has proven to be a good practice and is the reason that this book contains a CD of the standard operating procedures that appear in Section 4 for low, high and indoor challenge elements.

It is important that program managers and facilitators have a manual that outlines the policies, practices and procedures for their site. The comprehensiveness of such a manual may vary but it generally includes the following:

- **Site Logistics**
  - Course map
  - Keys/First aid kits/Emergency procedure directions
  - Meeting space/Phones/Restrooms/Equipment
- **A Guide to the Proper Operation of the Challenge Course Elements**
  - Proper set-up
  - Description of the task
  - Group size (can vary depending upon age, maturity, type of activity)
  - Facilitator's role
  - Spotting considerations
- **Emergency Action Plans**
  - Outline of specific procedures to be followed
  - Phone locations (cell, office) and the necessary numbers
  - Definition of types of emergencies, staff roles (see EAP specifics on following page)
- **Program Forms and Protocols**
  - Medical information/Liability
  - Accident/Incident/Near miss
  - Rope logs
  - Daily inspection/maintenance tips
  - White status board for communication of daily updates
- **Procedures to follow for Inclement Weather**

Additional information that may be part of a larger policies and procedures manual may include:
- List of staff, full and part time, who facilitate on the course and the types of activities each is qualified to lead, i.e., games, initiatives only, low and/or high elements
- An outline of the skill requirements of all staff relative to each activity area
- A copy of the most recent course inspection
- The staff training materials/packet used for skill refreshers and training

Emergency Action Plans

An emergency action plan (EAP) does the following:
1) Assigns responsibilities for action to be taken;
2) Preplans actions to be taken in different emergencies;
3) Identifies resources for responding to an emergency.[1]

An EAP is an important part of a program's local operating procedure. The staff needs to know the proper procedures to follow in the event of an emergency. Such procedures should be a regular part of staff training and the basic steps of such a procedure should be posted in obvious locations such as equipment sheds and staff rooms and included in first aid kits. While emergency action plans may vary depending upon the particulars of a program's location, some common procedures include:

- **ASSESSMENT OF THE SITUATION:** It should be clear prior to the start of a program who is responsible for assessing the situation in the event of an emergency. This responsibility generally lies with the lead trainer. If particular expertise (EMT, etc.) rests with another staff person, they should respond appropriately but under the direction of the lead trainer.

- **RESPONSIBILITIES FOR ACTION:** In addition to assessment of the situation, it should be clearly established who is responsible for the various actions to be taken, i.e., providing first aid, contacting EMS or plans for transport to a medical facility.

- **MANAGING THE GROUP:** Often the participants who are part of the group involved with the emergency need attention. Depending upon the severity of the situation it may be necessary to determine whether the program should continue. At a minimum, some form of debrief should take place to both share information and keep everyone informed and to allow participants to express their thoughts and feelings.

- **MAKING EMERGENCY CONTACT TO EMS:** Local operating procedures should clearly spell out the necessary steps for contacting EMS. Such procedures should be readily available. They can be posted in equipment sheds, staff rooms and included in first aid kits. Participant medical forms should also be available for EMS staff.

- **TRANSPORTING TO A MEDICAL FACILITY:** Local operating procedures should make clear how participants will be transported if necessary for the treatment of injuries.

- **NOTIFYING STAFF/FAMILY MEMBERS/MEDIA:** The need to contact other staff, family members of the participant or the media depends largely upon the severity of the accident or injury.

[1] Adapted from an article 2006 by Ian Wade, Director (Adventure Safety International/ Outward Bound International) in the Outdoor Network

Simple injuries treated by staff may only require that the appropriate paperwork be completed and one's program manager be notified. With programs involving minors, a follow-up call to a family member (even for minor injuries) can be a polite protocol that illustrates a caring practice on the part of your program.

Procedures to follow in the event of a severe accident or death should be clearly spelled out in the local operating procedure manual. Such situations should be dealt with by senior staff who are familiar with the established protocols.

Participant Readiness—Informed Consent

Some years ago a ten-year-old girl was attending a week-long session at a summer camp. When she returned home she was asked how she had enjoyed her week. She gave a somewhat standard response indicating that it was a lot of fun. She went on to say that they even did a little adventure stuff. Her parent inquired about the type of activities and she replied that they did trust falls. Her parent pursued the questioning by asking how it went. Her response was "Not good, they dropped the first two people!" The parent was slightly shocked. The girl continued by saying, "Don't worry, I was number three and we stopped at two."

This situation has always reminded me that people, in this instance, the girl and her parents, need to know what to expect from a program. Further information about the situation revealed that this particular camp was not an adventure camp and, in fact, made no reference to any adventure activities in their literature. However, during the week of staff training (general training not adventure training), prior to the beginning of camp, a number of adventure teambuilding activities were done with the staff. Trust falls was one of them. It turns out that the staff member that led the trust falls with the campers was merely trying to fill some free time utilizing the activity she had experienced during her staff orientation.

Let's take a moment to examine some of the pieces of this risk management puzzle that needed attention.

- participants had no idea that they were going to take part in an adventure activity that would include some risks and require a specific skill set such as spotting

- given that these participants were under age 18, parents should have been informed that such activities were going to be part of the camp's curriculum

- the purpose of the activity was not made clear to the participants

- the staff member had received no proper training in facilitating adventure activities

- the camp director and other supervisory staff were not aware that such an activity was taking place

- because adventure programming was not part of the camp curriculum, no local operating procedures existed for this type of programming

No doubt this list could be more extensive, but the point here is simply that participants need information. In this instance, given that the participants are minors, it would be the parents who are most in need of information. This situation is somewhat exaggerated because the camp was not in the

CAUGHT YOU THINKING #8:

We did trust falls at camp today.

How did it go?

Not good, they dropped the first two people!

adventure business, but assuming it was, campers (and parents) should have an understanding of what is expected of them and the nature of the activities in which they will be participating. Specifically, will there be games and initiatives that require some running around or will the program involve low and/or high challenge course elements that require climbing and a certain degree of comfort with heights? How will participants be expected to participate? A familiar and often used concept, called "Challenge by Choice,"[1] was developed by Project Adventure, Inc. many years ago. This concept helps a participant become an active decision maker regarding the degree of challenge she wants to accept as a participant (see the Glossary in the Appendix for further explanation and definition).

As we said in the introduction to this section, challenge course programs, like any other programs, have risks-both perceived and real. Fortunately the perceived risks outweigh the actual risks.

In the early years of adventure education, we felt it was only a matter of time before accidents and/or injuries resulting from challenge course programs would be viewed in the same way they are with other activities and sports. For example, when people play football it is inevitable that injuries will occur. It is considered a "part of the game." So much so, that most football programs are required to have an ambulance on site during the game. For whatever reason, accidents and injuries within adventure programs (even with the statistical proof that these programs have a very low rate of injury) will never attain the level of acceptability of sports that are more ingrained in our culture. It may be that the perception of risks associated with climbing and height simply outweighs the reality of the data regarding accidents.

Regardless of the mindset creating this apparent inequity, it is the responsibility of programs to be very forthright in their efforts to inform participants of the risks, perceived and real, and to have participants acknowledge these risks in writing. For most programs, but not all, this is done in the form of a release of liability statement.

1 The term Challenge by Choice is a registered service mark of Project Adventure, Inc.

Medical Screening and Participant Agreements

There have been two schools of thought about the appropriateness of gathering medical information from challenge course participants. One perspective is that it is best to collect very little information. This view expresses the belief that medical data are private and should be shared and interpreted only by people with professional medical training.

Another school of thought, and currently the more prevalent one, states that collecting basic medical information from participants about pre-existing conditions is useful to challenge course facilitators. If necessary, a facilitator with this background information could then advise participants with medical issues about appropriate levels of activity on the challenge course. All collected medical information must be held in confidence.

At High 5 we currently use two forms:

• An Adult Confidential Information, Waiver & Release of Liability for Challenge Course Activities

• A Student Confidential Information, Waiver & Release of Liability

Medical screening and participant agreements will vary from program to program, and from activity to activity with a program. The forms which follow are not, precisely, the forms now in use by High 5 but they may be useful as guides, to be reviewed by a program's legal counsel and modified according to local laws and the program's style, activities and participants. One program's forms will rarely, if ever, fit another program. You must seek the assistance of qualified legal counsel in this matter.

Accident/ Incident Tracking

In many ways an incident or near miss may serve as a warning or red flag regarding a local operating procedure or protocol that may need attention. Proper communication and reporting of such incidents are an important part of the management of any program.

For example, when the Giant Swing was being developed as a challenge course element, there were some kinks that needed to be worked out. This is generally true for any new element.

On one occasion involving the giant swing at our High 5 site, a staff person reported an incident that involved a participant receiving a rope burn. This was caused by the retriever line that was used to bring the haul rope back down to the ground after the participant had released.

The retriever line was initially connected to the figure-eight knot tied at the end of the haul rope, thereby placing it within the reach of the participant. In this instance the participant grabbed for the line right after pulling the release cord, resulting in the burn.

The critical eye of the staff member recognized the potential seriousness of this incident and responded with a solution that has worked well to this day. We now tie (and instruct this practice as well) a butterfly knot approximately four to six feet away from the end of the figure-eight knot and attach the retriever line to it thus placing it well out of the reach of the participant.

This was a simple solution but one that emerged from the thinking skills of a trained practitioner and resulted in the risks associated with this activity being significantly reduced.

Some programs use separate forms for accidents and incidents; others combine the information on the same form. The information on the sample forms in the Appendix is indicative of the type of information that should be collected. All staff should understand the proper use of the form and who it goes to when there is an occurrence of some kind.

Insurance

We are frequently asked questions regarding insurance for adventure programs. The good news is that it is much easier to find a good carrier now than it was years ago. As the field has grown, its acceptance and reputation as a viable and safe industry has grown as well. There are several insurance companies that have become involved with the industry and are quite familiar with adventure education programs. These companies tend to be easier to work with because they understand the concept of challenge courses and generally have a pool of clients for whom they are providing coverage. If your program is struggling with coverage issues because your provider is not familiar with adventure education programs, it can often help to put them in contact with one of the companies that are currently active in the industry.

The ACCT web site, **www.acctinfo.org**, frequently has helpful insurance information and resources.

As the beginning of this section stated, there are many pieces to the puzzle of program management that need to be thoughtfully put into place. Fortunately there are many resources to assist programs in completing this task. These resources can be found both within the adventure education field and in the greater field of risk management in general. These include:

- Training workshops specific to adventure programs and challenge course management. At High 5 we offer a workshop called Managing an Adventure Program. Other vendors offer similar workshops and these offerings will only increase as practitioner certification begins to become the norm within the field.
  Note: The growing importance of program management has been confirmed by its inclusion as a certification level for challenge course practitioners within the standards being developed through ACCT.

- The Association for Challenge Course Technology (ACCT) and the Association for Experiential Education (AEE) are quality professional organizations that provide resources for professionals in the field.

- Preston Cline of Adventure Management in Portsmouth, New Hampshire provides quality materials about risk management and specifics regarding emergency action plans. **www.adventuremanagement.com.**

PROGRAM IMPLEMENTATION

PROGRAM IMPLEMENTATION

As previously mentioned, we believe developing a good program design is the starting point for beginning a quality adventure education program. While having a program philosophy in place, a well trained staff and a challenge course and procedures that are up to date are all part of essential program readiness, these components in some ways are merely setting the stage for you to begin thoughtful program implementation.

In this section we will delve into this topic a bit more thoroughly, looking first at some typical start-up questions that can help in shaping a program's big picture goals. Several of these have been mentioned previously, but these questions capture them in a summarizing fashion. Then we will examine topics that are specific to individual program design such as assessment, before, during and after a program and various facilitation tips. The intent here is to broaden the understanding of the various components of program implementation.

SOME THOUGHT PROVOKING QUESTIONS TO CONSIDER WHEN STARTING AN ADVENTURE EDUCATION PROGRAM:

I'D LIKE TO DEVELOP AN ADVENTURE EDUCATION PROGRAM, WHERE DO I BEGIN?

We hear this question frequently and our standard response is: "What are the goals of your program? What are you trying to accomplish with your students, campers, etc.?" We can help you answer these questions and guide you about what you need to develop a successful adventure program. From game bags to initiative props to challenge course elements, the selection becomes easy when it is based upon your program goals.

Spending some time pondering these questions will ultimately save you time and money. And it will give you the right adventure tools to accomplish the job.

DO I NEED A CHALLENGE COURSE TO RUN A SUCCESSFUL ADVENTURE PROGRAM?

Quite simply, No! For the past thirty-plus years, many successful, exciting programs have been running their programs without a challenge course or with a minimal number of elements. There is some truth to the notion that there is nothing like a high-profile challenge course to get people jazzed about adventure learning; but it is not a pre-requisite to a quality program.

Most good programs spend a lot of quality time right on the ground and maximize the games and initiatives that are such a rich part of adventure education.

IF A CHALLENGE COURSE IS GOING TO BE PART OF MY PROGRAM, WILL I NEED A LOT OF MONEY TO BUILD IT?

Unfortunately, challenge courses-like everything else-have increased in cost over the years. We typically build courses in the range of $5,000 to $50,000. It has become pretty standard for programs that want a good size challenge course to build it in stages over a two to three-year period. This helps with the budget and can even support a progression and sequencing of activities that are consistent with curriculum goals and objectives.

HOW CAN I PROMOTE THE IDEA OF AN ADVENTURE EDUCATION PROGRAM TO STUDENTS, PARENTS, STAFF AND ADMINISTRATION?

One very successful method has been to sponsor an adventure awareness afternoon, evening or, better yet, a whole day. There is no better way to gain an understanding of adventure education than to experience it first hand. No amount of letters, brochures, videos or lectures can compare to actually doing some adventure activities with those you are trying to engage and influence.

DO YOU NEED SPECIAL INSURANCE TO RUN A CHALLENGE COURSE PROGRAM?

The simple answer is no. Most schools and organizations have existing insurance that will cover your adventure education program. Occasionally, camps or private institutions may need to add a rider to an existing policy to provide adequate coverage. On rare occasions, separate insurance has to be purchased.

HOW MUCH DOES IT COST TO MAINTAIN A CHALLENGE COURSE ON A YEARLY BASIS?

An annual inspection is recommended by High 5 and required by ACCT standards. Costs vary greatly depending upon the size of the course. They can range from $400 to $1,200 for the course inspection itself plus travel expenses. Repairs completed at the time of the inspection are extra and generally range from $500 to $1,500. As with anything, courses kept in good repair on a regular basis tend to have lower annual costs because repairs are not allowed to accumulate over the years resulting in a major one-time expense. On-going maintenance, such as spreading mulch, applying wood preservative, trimming overhanging dead limbs or removing dead trees take either internal resources or money to pay someone else to do this work.

High 5 and many other vendors regularly schedule annual inspections on a "swing." By this we mean a geographic swing through an area that has several locations in need of an annual inspection. We do them all at once and split the travel costs amongst all the sites. This can provide significant savings for each location.

HOW MUCH TRAINING IS REQUIRED TO RUN A CHALLENGE COURSE PROGRAM?

Training is the key component to any successful program. You can build a beautiful challenge course but it will remain just that until you have qualified staff to make good programs happen. We strongly recommend that staff have a minimum of a four to five-day skills based training workshop before taking on the demands of running a program. It's important to realize that four to five days is minimal. We regularly have people come to our training workshops that have attended multiple skill workshops over several years. They do this for several reasons, to refresh and sharpen technical skills, to spend time with other professionals in the field and to stay current with changes and trends. While being an adventure practitioner is not, as they say…brain surgery, it does require one to have a solid set of skills to assure safe and competent programming. We highly recommend that you view the training of good staff to be as important as building a beautiful challenge course.

WHERE CAN I GO FOR TRAINING?

There are many places you can go to find quality training workshops. The key here is to be particular. As with anything, make sure the vendor you choose is well qualified and is experienced training for the type of course you have at your site Ask around for recommendations from others. There's no better source of information than someone who has spent time with the organization that you're considering attending. Good quality, professional training is available. Make an effort to find the best match for the skills you need. The Association for Challenge Course Technology has a list of its Professional Vendor Members on its website. This is a very good resource for finding vendors who are in your geographic area and who are part of the largest professional organization in the field today.

CAUGHT YOU THINKING #9:

Can you train twenty of my staff to run the Zip Wire for our summer camp? I have about two hours available during our week-long staff training period!

PROGRAM ASSESSMENT AND DESIGN OVERVIEW

Thoughtfully designed programs blend a number of objectives. First, blending objectives assures that the program you deliver will more than likely meet the goals and needs of your participants. Secondly, activity selection based upon previously collected assessment criteria such as age, experience and ability reduce the risk of involving participants in inappropriate exercises. And, lastly, it gives you the opportunity to create a design that allows you to stay true to your own mission and philosophy, to do what you do best. This is as important for one-day programs as for eight-week curricula.

Delivering intentional programming is a good goal. We all get caught short at times, unprepared or frazzled, or surprised by a particularly unruly group and things still seem to work out. But the proverbial "shoot from the hip" style of programming will ultimately catch up with you. Be good to yourself and give it your best thought before the group or class shows up.

SPHERES OF SUCCESSFUL SEQUENCING

As the diagram indicates, the center of the bulls-eye is desirable but probably not always realistic. However, a little planning should keep you out of a lot of random programming or, worst yet, risky business.

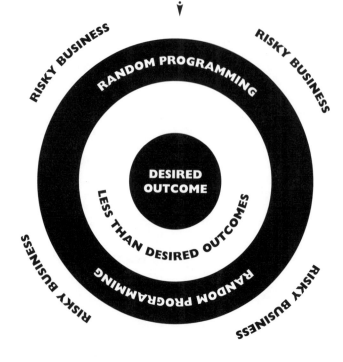

Pre-Program Assessment

Assessment is important. It is the critical tool that allows you to customize your program design to meet the specific needs of your group. Assessment can be a formal process that happens prior to meeting with a group. Such collected data is particularly important for groups that are new to the adventure experience. This period of inquiry also offers you the perfect opportunity to inform the group of the types of activities they may be engaged in during the program, the choices available around participation, the level of physical requirements (even if it is just walking to the challenge course) and proper clothing and footwear for the experience.

Questions that are typically asked in an assessment process include:

- Who is the group? What brings them together? (job, interest, club, class, team, special relationship etc.)

- Is this a newly formed group or one that has been together for a period of time?

- What are some of the general characteristics of the group? (Age, gender, physical abilities)

- What's the group size?

- Why have they specifically chosen the adventure experience?

- What are the goals and objectives for the workshop?

- Are they choosing to attend or is it mandatory?

- Are there any group norms, patterns, or behaviors that would be useful to know in advance in planning the design?

- Do any group members have specific physical disabilities, medical requirements or dietary restrictions?

Designing the Program

Designing and planning a workshop, session or class follows an initial assessment. Creating a workable sequence based upon the data gathered from the group is important for creating a program that energizes, progressively develops skills and infuses opportunities for maximizing reflection and learning. Further, thoughtful planning allows time for creativity and innovation and avoids the lock-step approach to adventure sequencing. With that said, sequencing is an important step to consider in the design of your program. Most educators would agree that basic concepts should be introduced before moving on to more complex ideas. In adventure education, this notion of incremental flow is also essential to creating meaningful learning experiences. Groups need to get to know each other before they can trust each other. Spotting techniques need to be learned before accessing challenge course elements. Simple initiative problems precede complicated challenges. Basic knots come before belay school and so on. Yet, there is no one specific method to sequence the adventure program. Instead, it is a dynamic process that takes into careful consideration the emotional and physical safety of the group, the educational goals of the group, the personality of the group, and the time and tools available to the leader and participants.

In creating the design, here are some questions that may help to guide and shape your program.

- What sequence of activities will best meet their stated goals and objectives?

- What activities will best suit their age, ability, level of experience, and commitment to the program?

- What activities do I enjoy that will add value to their experience?

- How much time will I need to allow in warm-ups and icebreakers to develop a sense of group?

- Given the age and experience of the group, how much time should be spent in active exercises and how much time spent in processing the experiences?

- What metaphors can I develop to customize the experience to the specific group?

- How can I build anticipation and surprise into the plan so that the group is always looking forward to the next activity?

- Is there plenty of variety in the choice of activity? Different levels of risk-taking? Different types of group interaction (dyads, triads, small group, large group)? Varying length of activities?

- Does the design have a clear beginning, middle, and end?

- What type of closure activity would be best for the group?

- Have I developed a plan that is within my skill base and level of knowledge?

Ongoing Assessment

On going assessment is also a useful tool. Group leaders need to continually observe their groups during programs to be sure that the selected activities are meeting the needs of the group and the situation. Individuals and groups will progress at different rates. A host of factors such as group size, prior experience, varying abilities, even the events on the way to the adventure program can all impact the learning that will take place. Learning how to read a group takes practice. The questions that follow help the facilitator to assess the preparedness of a group.

- How does the group get along? Are they respectful of each other?

- What is the level of caring in the group? Are they inclusive of each other? Are there cliques?

- Are there opportunities that will create success along the way?

- Are there any interactions between individuals that are disruptive to the group?

- What is the level of participation?

- Are they enthusiastic or resistant or bored?

- Are they cooperative or out for themselves?

- Do they listen well? Can they follow instructions?

- What are their abilities?

- Are they physically capable of doing the activities in the program or do the exercises need to be modified?

- Are there any medical restrictions or requirements?

- Does the group demonstrate a particular stage of development? Forming, storming, norming, or performing?

- Are there any limitations I can place on specific individuals (blindfolds, muted, use of only one arm, etc.) that can help the group progress or help address a desired learning outcome?

The amount of time required for a group to come together will vary. Trust may develop slowly in some groups. It is beneficial for the facilitator to have thought about some alternative activities if the group develops differently than expected. Remaining open and flexible to unexpected outcomes is a difficult but wonderful skill to cultivate. Be creative in your sequencing. Each activity is a valuable step forward in a process that focuses on growth and change.

CAUGHT YOU THINKING #10:

We'd like to bring our students for a day on your challenge course. We're only interested in the high elements.

Post-program Evaluation

It is important at the conclusion of a program to evaluate results.

• Did the program meet the desired outcomes?

• What were the reactions of the group?

• Were there signs of skill development?

• Does the group need follow-up?

Information collected either through written evaluations or verbal closing circles, provides first-hand reactions from participants about the program. This data is useful in both evaluating how the program was received by individuals and in deciding what next steps might be recommended for future work.

CAUGHT YOU THINKING #11:

What's your favorite

opening game

for groups?

Why does it work?

CHALLENGE COURSE ELEMENTS
LOW · HIGH · INDOOR

SECTION 4

THE LOW CHALLENGE COURSE

The moment of transition from field games and prop initiatives to the low challenge course is a time of high energy for participants. There is excitement and often anxiety about what is to come. What events are scheduled? How will our group manage them? How will I manage them? Do I have the necessary skills? Will I feel safe? Anticipating these reactions, the facilitator has her hands full, both making sure that the group is indeed ready for the low challenge course experience and giving them the preparation and confidence to move forward comfortably.

Managing safety is a top priority for the facilitator. Thoughtful preparation helps to ensure that all necessary groundwork has been covered. The following list of questions identifies some of the facilitator's basic responsibilities.

Facilitator Prep

READINESS OF THE GROUP

Is my group ready for the challenge course experience? Have I adequately prepared the participants for this next step with enough warm-ups and prop initiatives? Are they beginning to form a more cohesive unit? Does the group demonstrate a level of caring and support for each other? Is my planned sequence of activities still appropriate? Will my choice of elements continue to move the group towards their goals? (See Program Assessment & Design Overview in Section 3, Program Implementation)

COURSE INSPECTION

Have I inspected the elements that I intend to use? Is the area around, above and beneath the elements clear of obstacles? Have I checked for any evidence of insect nests (hornets, bees) in hanging tires or in ground holes? Has there been any severe weather on the course recently that may have resulted in damage to the elements? High winds? Lightning strikes?

EQUIPMENT FOR ELEMENTS

Do I have all the equipment I need to set up the elements properly? Is it in proper working order?

WEATHER

Have I checked the weather forecast? Have I made provisions for any extreme conditions (e.g. extra water for very hot days, extra clothing for cold days etc.)?

MEDICAL PREPAREDNESS

Am I prepared for medical emergencies? Do I know the medical emergency protocol for the site? Do I have access to information about participants with special medical conditions? Do I have a first aid kit that is appropriately stocked?

Facilitator's Role

What will be the most effective role for me with this group? Will I need to intervene often to keep the group on task or will I be able to let them work through their own process? To manage safety, will I need to be an active spotter in all activities or can I step back and sometimes supervise from the side? These can be difficult questions to answer. The bottom line is that the facilitator needs to pay attention to the group at all times, observing, watching the reactions and responses and then customizing the degree of intervention to the meet the needs of the group. In general, younger and less skilled audiences will require more direction.

Encouraging participants to play a key role in helping to manage safety on a challenge course is a fundamental aspect of effective adventure programming. Facilitators can solicit this support in the following ways.

OFFER CHOICE

Make participants aware of the schedule and nature of the activities at the start of the day. Participants given this information can then make decisions about which activities are appropriate for them. Invite group members to choose a level of participation which best suits their physical and emotional abilities. Offering choice has the potential for reducing safety-related problems as participants will opt to stay within their comfort zones. This concept is often referred to as Challenge by Choice, a term coined by Project Adventure, Inc.

FULL VALUE AGREEMENT

As a facilitator it is important to establish some basic ground rules and expectations for behavior at the start of a program. These guidelines set the tone for the experience and inform participants of their responsibilities to themselves and others throughout the program. Helping a group to set up behavioral norms that support and encourage positive interpersonal interactions increases the amount of sharing and deepens the group experience. These social contracts are often called Full Value Agreements (an agreement between participants, including the facilitator, that establishes group behavior norms). The agreement often becomes a valuable tool for the facilitator as it can serve as a reminder to the participants of their previous commitments to the group and to the issues of safety on the course.

AN INVITATION TO LEARN

Create an open, friendly environment that invites questions, comments and sharing. Make participants feel that they are an integral part of the learning process. For example, ask the group to think up alternative rules of play if a warm-up or game flops or lacks excitement. A solicitation for feedback from you will help participants feel valued and will encourage them to commit to the program and established social contracts. Further, show enthusiasm for any learning that occurs. Praise of genuine progress coupled with positive reinforcement provides motivation to the group to keep going and models the kind of "put-ups" that you want to encourage amongst group members. On the other hand, be there to supervise and intervene if negative actions or comments become disruptive to group members. Preserving a climate of emotional safety is as important as one of physical safety.

PROPER ATTIRE

Participants should come suitably dressed for the experience and the weather.

Advance notification of appropriate dress and footwear is essential. This should include a statement about leaving at home any jewelry or valuable articles that might get lost or broken. Necklaces, dangling earrings, rings etc. can be hazardous objects in some activities and should be removed before the start of an experience. The right attire increases a participant's enjoyment of the experience as well as increases their level of safety and comfort on the course. However, even with advance notice, many participants will show up unprepared. Students often think a sweatshirt is sufficient outerwear on a brisk morning. Professionals unaccustomed to the outdoors may show up in heels or sandals. Raingear is considered superfluous by the I-can-get-by crowd. Therefore, it is always a good idea to have some extra clothing around to hand out as needed.

The Art of Effective Facilitation

The challenge course is an effective tool for creating positive individual and group change and growth, but it is only a tool or physical structure. The power of the challenge course lies in the thoughtful facilitation of this valuable tool and model for learning.

Facilitation is the process of guiding participants through opportunities to learn and grow and create positive change in their group. It is an art developed through a blend of training, experience, observing others, practice and intuition. It is improved upon when practitioners take the time to develop their skills repertoire and personal style as a facilitator.

Here are some ideas for practicing the art of facilitation:

- DON'T RUSH.
  Take the time up front to help your participants create a positive environment for learning, through careful sequencing of activities that "warm up the group" and build trust progressively. Empower them to create positive norms using tools such as the full value agreements mentioned previously (under "Facilitator's Role")—and remember to check in regularly on the group's "climate." This time spent up front developing a positive environment pays off with more in-depth participation by group members later.

- REMEMBER THAT ONE OF THE FUNDAMENTAL ASPECTS OF EXPERIENTIAL EDUCATION IS TO GIVE CONTROL TO PARTICIPANTS
  and allow them to learn through the process of struggling through problems together.[1] A challenge course, by its very nature, is a series of problems to solve. Remember to let this happen—sometimes facilitators are tempted to jump in too early when a group is struggling through a problem—allow for some laboring with problems or conflict as this is where the learning takes place. Obviously there is a fine balance between labor and paralyzing frustration; you as an educator have to figure out that appropriate balance along with your participants. Just remember people learn more when given questions rather than answers.

- LOOK AT YOURSELF AS A GUIDE RATHER THAN TEACHER
  and center of knowledge and direction. Create opportunities for group members to take leadership and direction. As the group builds together you can take less of a leadership role, allowing participants to take more responsibility for their learning and therefore a stronger sense of personal accomplishment for their successes.

1 Cain, James, Cummings, Michelle, and Stanchfield Jennifer. *A Teachable Moment: A Facilitator's Guide to Activities for Processing, Debriefing, Reviewing and Reflecting*. Dubuque, IA: Kendall/Hunt Publishing Co., 2005.

CAUGHT YOU THINKING #12:

Has it become common practice for adventure programs to have participants wear climbing helmets while doing the 12' Initiative Wall?

- **USE YOUR CREATIVITY.**
  Keep facilitation interesting for you and your participants, use interesting props, humor or story lines. Mix up your methods to meet the differing learning styles of your participants.

- **YOUR ATTITUDE MAKES ALL THE DIFFERENCE.**
  Participants really pick up on their leader's attitudes, demeanor and expectations. We often communicate more than we realize in our body language and tone. If we expect the best of participants they will usually perform their best. A facilitator's positive attitude is contagious. So make sure you really believe in what you are doing—if there is activity you don't feel comfortable with, or a method you don't believe in your participants will pick up on that and likely won't "buy in" either.

- **BE WILLING TO TRY NEW THINGS.**
  Don't be afraid if an activity doesn't work out as you planned—that is where key learning can occur.

- **BE INTENTIONAL; BUT ALSO BE WILLING TO LET GO OF YOUR PLAN**
  to meet the changing needs of the group. Be prepared for the unexpected and take advantage of teachable moments.

- **LEARN FROM OTHERS.**
  Co-lead: Good facilitators learn new activities, tricks and methods for dealing with challenging group situations from each other. Create opportunities to co-lead with another facilitator; you will learn a great deal from their new ideas and from the co-creative aspect of sharing your own as you plan together.

- **BE CULTURALLY SENSITIVE.**
  Try to keep in mind cultural or social differences in language and slang terms when you present activities. Some activity names could be unknowingly offensive or hurtful.

- **CREATE LASTING LESSONS.**
  Be thoughtful about presenting reflective techniques to carry lessons forward to the next session or to future life situations.

- **CLOSURE IS IMPORTANT.**
  Be thoughtful about how you end a program or day's experience. Think about what you want the group to leave with and plan a final reflective or celebration activity accordingly to tie it all together.

- **TAKE TIME TO REFLECT**
  as a facilitator after a program is over on what worked well and what you would do differently next time.

For more ideas and resources for developing the art of group facilitation, see Jennifer Stanchfield, *Tips & Tools for the Art of Group Facilitation*, Wood N Barnes publishing, 2007.

Skills for the Low Challenge Course

TEACHING SPOTTING

Facilitators should be thoroughly familiar with the operational guidelines for each challenge course element prior to use. Each element has its own spotting nuances. The techniques for managing safety on traversing and swinging elements are different. Before introducing the group to any elements, participants should be taught the requisite skills necessary to safely engage in the activity. However, the first step begins with the introduction to the basic skill of spotting.

SPOTTING SKILLS

Spotting is one of the most critical skills taught on the challenge course. It prepares both a group and its members for the emotional and physical experiences that are to follow. Up to this point, in a standard sequence of adventure programming, a group has likely been involved in a series of ice-breakers, warm-up games and possibly portable problem-solving exercises. The focus has been on getting to know each other, discovering the keys to help the group function effectively and establishing acceptable boundaries and group norms. As well, participants may have learned to rely on each other for ideas, feedback and cooperation, but it is unlikely that they have experienced a reliance on each other for physical safety. The introduction of spotting introduces a heightened level of interaction. The tone in the group frequently changes when participants realize that they will be both trusting others for their safety and reciprocally having others trust them. Often, acceptance of this additional responsibility becomes a turning point for groups. Therefore, the training for spotting should be a careful and thoughtful process. At the same time, it allows the facilitator an opportunity to assess the group. How are the participants reacting to the spotting exercises? Do they listen attentively? Are they serious with each other? Are they ready to move on to activities on the challenge course?

The prevention of injury is the goal of spotting. Some basic techniques for teaching spotting are as follows.

- **DEMONSTRATE A PROPER SPOTTING POSITION:** hands up in a ready position, feet sturdily placed and attention focused on the participant. Emphasize that spotters should be prepared to follow the movement of the participant, adjusting their spotting position to best respond to any potential fall.

- **EXPLAIN THAT SPOTTING DOES NOT NECESSARILY MEAN CATCH-ING**. Its purpose is to prevent injury by providing physical support, particularly to the head and upper body. It is important to point out the difficulty of stopping dynamic movement, even in a short fall.

- UNDERSTAND THAT SPOTTING SHOULD BE TAUGHT IN A PROGRESSIVE SEQUENCE. Begin with practice spotting activities that reinforce proper technique. A traditional progression usually starts with trust activities such as the Maze or a Sherpa Walk and moves through an explanation of spotting to a Two Person Trust Lean to Willow in the Wind.

- ESTABLISH A CLEAR AND AGREED UPON PATTERN OF COMMUNICATION between spotters and fallers. A meaningful verbal exchange alerts spotters to the movements of a participant. A common version of this communication goes as follows:

Participant:	**Spotter ready?**
Spotter:	**Ready. (Use of first names personalizes the experience)**
Participant:	**Ready to step up (walk, fall, etc.)**
Spotter:	**Step Away, (walk, fall)**

- CREATE OPPORTUNITIES FOR SPOTTERS TO ROTATE POSITIONS and/or responsibilities. Know that spotting can be tiring. Check in periodically with spotters to see how they are doing.

- HELP YOUR GROUP TO SEE SPOTTING AS A SHARED RESPONSIBILITY. In this way, larger group members do not get singled out as the safest spotters or the hardest one to protect. Encourage positive support and cheerleading for participants.

- KNOW THAT SPOTTING TOO CLOSELY MAY SIGNIFICANTLY REDUCE A PARTICIPANT'S CHALLENGE LEVEL on an element and ultimately her feelings of accomplishment. Help spotters find the balance between being effective and safe yet not overly protective in their spotting roles.

- FURTHER, AS A FACILITATOR, RECOGNIZE THAT YOU WILL NEED TO SUPERVISE SPOTTERS APPROPRIATELY, reminding them of correct positioning as needed.

- AS FACILITATORS, IT IS IMPORTANT TO BE FAMILIAR WITH THE SPOTTING REQUIREMENTS for all your challenge course elements. Spotting on a traversing cable element requires different techniques than spotting on a swinging event.

- FURTHER, KNOW THAT YOU CAN ALWAYS EXCEED THE MINIMUM SPOTTING REQUIREMENTS as outlined in the operating guidelines in this manual. Inexperienced or less mature groups may benefit from additional spotters. Extra spotters may also give waiting participants a more active role.

REFLECTION ACTIVITIES

It is valuable to spend time at the end of each activity reflecting upon the challenge or challenge course initiative. The insights gained in the debrief session give the group a chance to note any opportunities for improvement related to safety, group management issues or violations of their Full Value Agreement. As importantly, the period of reflection offers a moment of celebration for personal and group successes, often fueling the motivation for moving forward to new and potentially more challenging events.

THE VALUE OF REFLECTION

Reflection is one of the most important aspects of quality challenge course facilitation. The educational philosopher John Dewey (1933), known as one of the forefathers of experiential education, believed that in order to truly learn from experience there must be time for reflection. Recent brain research on how people learn best affirms this idea that time spent helping a group reflect (often called processing or debriefing) will help learners make connections between their educational experiences and real life situations. The challenge course can be a powerful educational tool. Reflection is what brings the learning experiences on the challenge course to life.

Spending time throughout a challenge course program to process will increase outcomes. Insights gained in debriefing a group challenge can help the group learn from conflict and give the group a moment to celebrate personal and group successes. The process of reflecting on group achievements can fuel the motivation for moving forward to new and more challenging events.

The quality of the group's experience can increase with the group having the opportunity to note any safety or group management issues, areas they need to focus on or any violations of their full value agreements. Through the process of group reflection, you as facilitator will be able to evaluate your group's progress towards its goals. You can better assess the changing needs of the group to maximize positive outcomes and take advantage of teachable moments.

There is no one prescribed way to process or reflect with a group. Using a variety of techniques and activities that eventually give learners the power to take the lead in reflection is an effective way to approach processing. When facilitators blend both activity and discussion and engage groups with a variety of processing methods they are more likely to reach the different learning styles of the group members.

Reflective activities, ranging from conversational prompts such as dice with questions, partner sharing and the use of metaphorical symbols and props to journaling, allow for the interpretation of the experience to fall on the group rather the facilitator. The use of symbols and metaphor can enhance meaningful reflection and discussion between group members and build participants' comfort with reflective practice.

Reflection is a skill that is developed with practice. Participants are more comfortable and willing to engage if processing activities are thoughtfully sequenced, and when participants are feeling empowered by having choice and control about when they share.[1]

Often facilitators get caught in situations where processing feels forced. This often happens when facilitators lead a question-and-answer session that their group might not be ready for. It takes time for many people to get comfortable sharing with the group. Start with simple non-threatening reflective techniques such as a one-word reflection on an activity. Allow hesitant group members to pass. Then incrementally bring in other reflective tools and methods to increase the group's comfort and ability to process more deeply. The ideal state is to eventually get the group to the point where they process spontaneously on their own after an activity without the facilitator leading discussion.[2]

Facilitators looking to increase their effectiveness with group reflection can find a variety of useful facilitation guides, reflection activity books, tools, props and workshops available in our field (see the Bibliography on page 204). Remember to plan ahead and leave time and opportunity in your program for reflection. Reflection brings out the full value of challenge course activities, enhances the quality and meaning of your program and activities and optimizes the outcomes for your participants. It is what brings the valuable lessons learned on the challenge course to life.

1 Stanchfield, Jennifer *Tips & Tools for the Art of Group Facilitation.* 2007 Wood N Barnes Publishing
2 Cain, Cummings and Stanchfield *A Teachable Moment: A Facilitator's Guide to Activities for Processing, Debriefing, Reviewing and Reflection.* 2005 Kendall Hunt Publishing

OPERATING PROCEDURES FOR LOW CHALLENGE COURSE ELEMENTS AND INITIATIVES

The following section on Low Challenge Course Elements and Initiatives details the standard operating procedures for many of the low elements built by High 5 Adventure Learning Center. It is important to recognize that individual challenge courses vary and that basic operational practices may require modification to meet the unique features of each course.

- A-FRAME
- ALL ABOARD
- DO I GO
- FIDGET LADDER
- HICKORY JUMP
- HOUR GLASS
- LORD OF THE RINGS
- LOW MULTI-LINE TRAVERSE
- THE MAZE
- MOHAWK WALK
- NITRO CROSSING
- PORTHOLE (HOLE IN ONE)
- SEAGULL SWING TO THE SWINGING LOG
- SPIDER'S WEB
- SWINGING LOG
- SWINGING TIRES
- TEAM TROLLEY TRAVERSE
- TP SHUFFLE
- TRIANGLE TENSION TRAVERSE
- TROLLEYS
- TRUST FALL
- THE WALL
- WHALE WATCH
- WILD WOOSEY

USER GUIDE:

Elements in this section are listed alphabetically.
The information about each element is subdivided into the following categories.

DEGREE OF DIFFICULTY

There are three levels:

BASIC—*Introductory Challenges: In a sequence of activities, these elements would normally follow warm-ups, trust activities and perhaps some portable initiatives. Participants need basic spotting knowledge.*

INTERMEDIATE—*Moderate Challenges: Groups should have good spotting skills as well as a demonstrated ability to work successfully together.*

ADVANCED—*Higher Level Challenges: These elements may require focused spotting and the ability to manage dynamic movement. Initiatives might be complex requiring good problem-solving skills.*

ELEMENT NAME
Brief description of the element.

TASK
A brief description of the objective for each challenge. Set-up instructions may be included with more unique elements.

GROUP SIZE
Suggests ideal working numbers for each element.

SPOTTING CONSIDERATIONS
This section includes the spotting instructions for each element. It is important that facilitators cover each point with their groups. A facilitator may choose to add additional operational instructions for an element, particularly if in her judgment, an activity warrants extra guidelines.

FACILITATOR'S ROLE
Included are safety reminders, tips to help an activity run more smoothly and special considerations for specific elements. All of these are in addition to the following general management responsibilities that are required before running any event.

- *Checking the ground for unsafe ground cover, looking for branches broken at eye level, and inspecting for widow makers above.*

- *Inspecting the mechanics of each element to be sure it is in good working order. That would include a visual examination, where possible, of key components.*

- *Clearly presenting the problem, reviewing the spotting requirements and answering any questions before the group begins the task.*

- *Being aware of the needs of participants. This means ongoing assessment of the group's progress. Appropriate schedule adjustments to better suit the group's needs are good programming practices.*

VARIATIONS
Alternative ways of using or presenting an element.

A-FRAME

This is a unique initiative that requires a group to move a wooden A-frame from point A to point B with one participant standing in the A-frame. The A-frame constructed of 2 x 4 lumber is about 10' high and has 4 ropes attached to various points of the apparatus.

TASK

The objective is to move the A-frame about 30' from point A to point B with one person standing aboard in the center of the A.

- The A-frame must maintain at least one point of contact with the ground at all times.

- Only one person stands on the A-frame. She must try to avoid contact with the ground.

- The remainder of the group manages the ropes to keep the A-frame upright at all times. Through coordinated pulling and tension on the ropes, the group can move the A-frame forward in a series of rocking-motion steps. The A-frame participant can assist the movement with shifts in her body weight.

- The guide ropes cannot touch the ground.

SPOTTING CONSIDERATIONS

- Make sure that the rope handlers are at least 10' away from the A-frame itself.

- Instruct the rope handlers to maintain enough constant tension on the ropes to keep the A-frame upright at all times.

- The rider of the A-frame may be individually spotted. Instruct the spotter to be alert to the movements of the apparatus. Other group members should remain outside the rope area (near the A-frame) during the activity.

- This activity is best done outside on a grassy surface. The legs of the A-frame may slip on a gymnasium floor.

FACILITATOR'S ROLE

Continue to monitor group and intervene if the alignment of ropes would allow the A-frame to fall forwards or backward.

DEGREE OF DIFFICULTY

Basic

The numbers that can fit on the platform will be determined by the size of the base and the size of the people.

DEGREE OF DIFFICULTY

Basic.
This is a good
introductory exercise.

ALL ABOARD

A portable wooden platform (usually 2' x 2' or 3' x 3') that can be used as an element in itself or as a landing base for activities such as the Nitro Crossing, Do I Go or Trolleys.

TASK

To have a group of participants try to fit as many people as possible on the designated platform for a given period of time. To be truly all aboard, no body parts should have contact with the ground.

SPOTTING CONSIDERATIONS

• Do not allow participants to sit on each other's shoulders.

• Encourage the group to actively spot while participants are loading the platform. The bulk mass of bodies can easily become unstable, potentially resulting in a group fall.

• Ask people to step down and away from the platform if they feel they are about to fall.

FACILITATOR'S ROLE

• Make sure the platform is placed in an open area free from obstacles.

• Spot as needed when the whole group climbs aboard.

• All Aboard platforms can be very slippery when wet. Exercise caution and use additional spotters as needed.

VARIATIONS

Have the group try the exercise non-verbally.

DO I GO

Four 2' x 2' platforms are evenly placed around the plumb line of a swing rope. To illustrate, picture the number five face of a die. The rope is represented by the center dot of the number five. The remaining four dots represent the platforms.

TASK

- Have a group distribute themselves evenly on the four platforms. If your group numbers more than sixteen, you may want to use larger platforms.

- The object is for each person to swing to another platform without touching the ground. A turf touch results in sending the offending swinger back to the platform from which she started. Anyone else that happens to get knocked off a platform must also return to her originating platform.

SPOTTING CONSIDERATIONS

- As all participants are usually positioned on one of the four platforms, the instructor normally manages spotting. However, additional spotters should be asked to help as needed.

- Participants should be cautioned against swinging too hard and too fast.

- Spot participants carefully as they are stepping into or out of the swing rope loop.

FACILITATOR'S ROLE

- Be mindful of the varying upper arm strengths of the participants. Encourage use of the foot loop as needed. Proactively spot as needed.

- Do I Go platforms can be very slippery when wet. Exercise caution and use additional spotters as needed.

GROUP SIZE

Twelve to sixteen participants work well. More can be accommodated with larger platforms.

DEGREE OF DIFFICULTY

Intermediate. Effective spotting is required for participants swinging onto platforms.

FIDGET LADDER

The multi-runged wood and rope fidget ladder is an element that tests balance and precision. Suspended between two points, the ladder is set at such an angle that its lowest end is generally two to three feet off the ground and its highest end eight to nine feet above the ground.

TASK

An individual once set on the low end of the ladder attempts to move upwards while remaining in a balanced position on hands and feet.

SPOTTING CONSIDERATIONS

• Spotters need to be informed about the quick movement of the Fidget Ladder. Once weighted, the ladder can quickly flip upside down swinging in a wide arc as it turns. Spotters must stand clear of the ladder's turning radius.

• Spotters should hold the fidget ladder still while a participant mounts the ladder.

• Spotting practices for the fidget ladder vary. Effective techniques are as follows:

– For indoor use, gym mats placed underneath the ladder can successfully cushion falls. If a gym mat is used, one to two spotters should be placed at the high end of the fidget ladder ready to protect a falling participant from having contact with the high end support structure. Spotters should also be placed along the sides with arms in a spotting position to protect a climber who may fall off the Fidget Ladder. Care should be exercised to stay clear of the rungs in the event of a quick flip.

– For both indoor and outdoor use, a cargo net made of either rope or webbing can be slung lengthwise underneath the fidget ladder. This safety net is managed by a group of spotters who each hold one section of the net. The spotting net must be wide enough to allow room for spotters to remain clear of the element. If a fall occurs, spotters pull back on the net providing enough tension to keep the participant from having contact with the ground.

– In both cases, participants must be told to hold on to the element with both hands if a fall occurs. This keeps the head in an upright and protected position.

VARIATIONS

Offer the Fidget Ladder in varying degrees of difficulty. The easiest is slithering up the ladder like a snake using the whole body. More difficult is allowing use of knees, hands and feet. The most difficult is an attempt with just hands and feet.

GROUP SIZE

One individual attempts the ladder surrounded by a group of spotters.

DEGREE OF DIFFICULTY

Advanced. Experienced and reliable spotters are needed for this dynamic element.

HICKORY JUMP

A trapeze, (suspended ball, Velcro strip or other target) hung from two cables approximately eight feet above the ground, provides a target for a jumper. The launch is made from a graduated series of steps or wooden posts.

TASK

A participant stands on one of a series of graduated steps or poles that have been placed perpendicular to and directly back from the trapeze.

With spotters in place and ready, a participant dives forward in an attempt to catch the trapeze or touch the target. Additional jumps may include attempts from progressively more distant stumps.

SPOTTING CONSIDERATIONS

- Participants need to have a clear understanding of how to catch lateral movement (a diving person) versus vertical movement (Trust Fall). See Trust Fall description.

- Participants need to know that the catching position for the *Hickory Jump* is different from the *Trust Fall* positioning.

- Spotting instructions should include the following:

  – Arms extended and bent at the elbows with palms up in a line as if spotting for the *Trust Fall*.

  – Feet are in stride position. Foot farthest from the platform and the faller is extended forward.

  – Knees are flexed with the spotter having made a quarter turn towards the jumper.

  – Spotters are shoulder to shoulder (Velcro shoulders) to ensure a strong and tight catching bed of arms.

  – All attention is focused on the jumper throughout the activity.

GROUP SIZE

A jumper requires a minimum of eight spotters. More than eight spotters are often desirable.

DEGREE OF DIFFICULTY

Advanced. Experienced and reliable spotters are needed for this event.

- Spotters must be in agreement that A JUMPER WILL NEVER SWING THROUGH after catching the trapeze. This is crucial for the jumper's safety. The jumper is first briefly caught in the spotters' line, then assisted into an upright standing position (whether they catch the trapeze or not).

- Caution jumpers to refrain from kicking or pumping legs and feet while jumping for the trapeze.

- Help spotters realize that catchers who are positioned nearest the shortest stumps need to be aware that part of their function is protect a jumper's shins and feet from contact with those stumps.

COMMUNICATION

Jumper   **(initiates the commands by saying,) "Spotters ready?"**

Spotter: **"Ready to catch (insert jumper's name)."**

Jumper: **"Jumping."**

Spotters: **"Jump away!"**

FACILITATOR'S ROLE

- Kick the jump stumps laterally to ensure their soundness.

- Present the task and specifically review spotting requirements. Make sure all jewelry, pencils, large belt buckles, and the like are removed from the jumper. Have spotters remove watches and bracelets etc.

- Use spotters as needed for jumpers mounting or walking up the stumps.

- Monitor the fatigue level of the spotters. Be prepared to stop the event if the spotters are getting tired or losing their concentration.

HOUR GLASS

Two lengths of 3/4" Multi-line rope with ends connected to four staples placed in support trees at 6" and 7' from the ground. The ropes are set in such a way that they intersect to form a large "X". If you connect the two ropes where they cross, the challenge is substantially reduced.

TASK
The object is for a participant to make her way from one support tree to another on the crossed ropes without touching the ground.

SPOTTING CONSIDERATIONS
- Keep your eyes on the participant's mid-section at all times to watch for movement. If the position of her waist quickly shifts, a fall may be imminent. Don't be distracted by arm, head and leg gyrations.

- Keep your hands and arms ready, but don't hold participants in position on the rope.

- Falls happen suddenly. Spotters must be prepared at all times.

FACILITATOR' ROLE
- The Hour Glass is more difficult than most low challenge course challenges. Introduce this element when a group is ready to take on a greater challenge.

- Emphasize spotting by having at least four people spot for each participant.

- Encourage participants to try more than one time. This event lends itself to practice and perseverance.

VARIATIONS:
A third rope can be added between the two bottom staples. In essence, the element becomes a low Pirate's Crossing (see high elements section). This adaptation of the Hour Glass makes it an easier element.

GROUP SIZE
No mandated limits. Too large a group may reduce the number of opportunities for repeated tries.

DEGREE OF DIFFICULTY

Advanced. The Hour Glass requires alert and reliable spotting as falls are fast and frequent.

LORD OF THE RINGS

Built in a circle of trees or poles, this element is formed by cables of varying lengths that radiate out from a central hub like spokes on a bicycle wheel. Some of the trees may have placements for Tension Traverse ropes. Strung between two of the trees is an overhead Multi-line rope which can be adjusted by a Prusik knot to hang at various heights to alter the difficulty of the element.

TASK

- Participants each begin on a separate cable at an outer tree or pole. The challenge is for each participant to end up in a new "starting position" without falling off the cable. Suggested rules are as follows:

  - No props are allowed other than the fixed ropes. Coats, shoe strings, and other clothing are off limits. One exception might be to allow a group to use a prop to retrieve the overhead line. It can be a long reach for younger audiences.

  - If a participant steps off the cable, she would return to her starting position.

SPOTTING CONSIDERATIONS

- Spotters should be used as needed as participants exchange places on the cable.

- Spotters need to be aware of the nature of a fall from the Tension Traverse sections. A falling participant will tend to fall back towards the starting point, particularly if they maintain contact with the rope. To be effective, two spotters need to position themselves accordingly, *one half step back toward the starting point*. (For more details, see Triangular Tension Traverse)

- Participants should be advised to help themselves by stepping down from the cable if a fall is imminent and unavoidable.

- Participants should not move independently along the cable, i.e. without contact with another participant or a Tension Traverse rope.

- Rapid traversing movement on the cable should be discouraged.

FACILITATOR'S ROLE

• The ground should be checked for rocks and stumps that may need extra spotting.

• Encourage participants to ask for spotters if feeling unstable.

VARIATIONS

• Limit the use of the overhead rope to only one member of the group at one time.

• Require all participants to move through the center hub on their way to their final destination.

GROUP SIZE

6-20 participants would allow for adequate spotting and participation.

DEGREE OF DIFFICULTY

Basic to Intermediate
The closer the ropes are
hung, the easier the traverse.

LOW MULTI-LINE TRAVERSE

Two cables are strung parallel to the ground, respectively at two and fifteen feet off the ground. Multi-line ropes of varying lengths are suspended at fixed intervals from the upper cable. This activity often serves as one segment of a Mohawk Walk.

TASK

An individual attempts to walk the length of the bottom cable using the hanging ropes for balance and support. Another variation is to have two participants start from opposite ends and try to meet or pass in the center. This can also be an initiative for an entire group—moving everyone from point A to B.

SPOTTING CONSIDERATIONS

• Participants should ask for spotters as needed. Two to four spotters can follow alongside each traversing participant to aid when necessary.

• Participants should step off the cable if a fall is imminent or if they feel fatigued.

VARIATIONS

The crossing may also be attempted in pairs.

THE MAZE

The Maze is just that, a maze composed of a series of rope hand lines attached to trees. These lines form an intricate network from which there is only one exit. A group's goal is to find their way out of the Maze.

Generally, groups are led in blindfold fashion to the Maze area to preclude any visual scouting of the problem.

TASK
- If groups are first blindfolded and then led to the Maze, encourage them to stand quietly to wait for someone to come and lead them into the Maze.

- Next, place people as efficiently as possible throughout the Maze, keeping up a constant supportive chatter. Make sure that all participants have hand contact with a portion of the Maze line.

- When the entire group is within the Maze and each person has a Maze cord in hand, explain that it is up to the group to exit the Maze without stooping beneath the cord, stepping over the cord, cutting the cord, untying the cord, etc. Assure them that there is indeed an exit and that when a person physically passes through the exit, someone will tap her on her shoulder as a signal that she is free of the Maze confines.

- Communication between group members is not only allowed, it is key for sharing information. However, once out of the Maze, all communication from the exited member must cease.

- If an exited participant, after observing what's going on within the Maze, wants to altruistically reenter and help teammates, that person is re-blindfolded, turned around a couple of times, then reinserted by a facilitator.

- That newly knowledgeable person cannot talk (optional), but can make loud sounds, and is allowed physical guiding contact with the participants remaining within the Maze.

- When everyone has exited or the exercise is brought to an end, allow some time for the now sighted participants to appreciate where they have been by walking them through the Maze and giving them an opportunity to share their individual sightless experiences.

GROUP SIZE

An ideal size is between 10-20 participants.

DEGREE OF DIFFICULTY

Basic.

SPOTTING CONSIDERATIONS

• Caution participants to walk slowly with their free hand in a bumper up position to avoid sudden contact with trees or other Maze connector points.

• Remind participants that the Maze cord must always be held by at least one hand, i.e. no wandering aimlessly within the Maze confines. If someone chooses to risk a short journey from the rope, have them have contact with another participant's hand.

FACILITATOR'S ROLE

• Check the area first to be sure that there are no branches broken off at eye level, vertical sticks protruding up from the ground, or any obstacles which could injure a participant.

• Assuage fears by indicating that the blindfolds can be removed as needed at any time. If wearing blindfolds seems problematic for the group, simply suggest that the group commit to keeping their eyes closed throughout the exercise.

VARIATIONS

• Have the group attempt the task non-verbally.

• Don't tell the participants what they are looking for, but say, for example: "You'll know when you've found the treasure."

• Indicate that the group has to stay together and cannot separate.

• Hang an object from one of the lines in the Maze. Ask the group to find and retrieve that object in addition to the primary task of exiting the Maze.

MOHAWK WALK

A Mohawk Walk is comprised of a series of low cable challenges strung between trees or poles that sequentially present a complex task for participants.

TASK
For the group as a whole to traverse the entire length of a series of cables— from point A to Z— without making contact with the ground. A variety of hand-lines may be installed at various points to create interest for the task.

SPOTTING CONSIDERATIONS
- If a fall is imminent, have participants agree to step off the cable and not pull off other participants.

- Have participants agree to work together to avoid individuals making solo attempts without the group's consideration.

- Use group members where spotting is necessary. Group members may step off the Mohawk Walk at resting points to serve as additional spotters.

- Have participants agree not to run on the cable or dive for fixed points or trees.

- Spot more difficult sections of the Mohawk as needed. This would include any swings and/or key transition moves from one cable to another. Also, spot rock outcroppings or uneven areas of ground.

VARIATIONS
- If a member of the group falls off, have that person return to wherever the end of the group is located or to the beginning of the challenge.

- Have the whole group return to the beginning of the problem if any one member falls off. (Better bring along lunch for this variation as it can lead to a rather long initiative problem.)

- Set a predetermined number of allowed falls before the activity begins and allow fallers to get back on at the spot from where they fell.

- If time is a concern, use only three or four sections of the element.

GROUP SIZE
- 10-12 participants are ideal.

- If your group is bigger, divide them in half and have each of the smaller groups start on opposite ends.

DEGREE OF DIFFICULTY

Intermediate to Advanced. This depends upon the difficulty of the individual cable elements.

- Offer props to the group. Possibilities are:

  – **A CRUTCH**: a real one— at the beginning of the problem with the proviso that the crutch can make contact with the ground, but can only move forward never backward. Use of the crutch is disallowed if it touches the ground behind its most forward contact.

  – **A HULA HOOP:** a tool that could be used just once in the activity to create a magic island on the ground. Participants would be allowed to step into this space.

  – **A LENGTH OF ROPE** that could be strung up as an additional hand line. Knots tied by participants should be checked by facilitators.

NITRO CROSSING

A swing rope with an attached optional prusik loop is suspended from a hanging cable. As this is an element that challenges a group to swing from Point A to Point B, boundary markers can be positioned horizontally at the beginning and end of the problem, usually about a foot off the ground.

TASK

For an entire group to swing across a designated area without touching the intervening area by:

- First obtaining the dangling rope using any resource found within the group (no sticks, ropes, etc.). No leaping or diving is permitted.

- Transporting across the area a container filled with water (nitro) without spilling a drop. The group may elect to make the carry at any point during the exercise.

SPOTTING CONSIDERATIONS

- Participants should agree not to use excessive force to swing members across the no-touch area.

- Participants should agree to not dive or jump for the rope.

- Participants should agree to encourage and support each person's swinging effort. Participants should not be coerced into trying this activity.

- Encourage careful spotting during the dismount if a group member uses the loop in the end of the rope.

- Disallow any wrapping of the rope around the hands as it may result in rope burns.

FACILITATOR'S ROLE

- Encourage participants to take a trial swing before the activity starts to see if they can support their own weight. If any group member has difficulty with the swing, adjust the task rules to accommodate their level of participation.

- Be prepared to spot participants as needed. Recognize that it is difficult to spot individuals in mid-swing. Also, pay special attention to participants who use the foot loop to make sure they step out cleanly from the loop.

GROUP SIZE

10-16 participants are ideal.

DEGREE OF DIFFICULTY

Basic to Intermediate

VARIATIONS

SWING ABOARD

This activity is essentially the same as the Nitro Crossing except that the designated landing area is on a 3' x 3' platform. Participants must be alert to falling off the platform. Do not allow participants to get on each other's shoulders.

DISC JOCKEYS

This is again similar to the two previous activities but now the landing is in a series of hoops (old bike tires work well) or on discs. There is one hoop or disc per participant. Although guidelines vary for this event, participants essentially must remain in the hoop in which they initially land.

Spotting considerations for both variations follow.

SPOTTING CONSIDERATIONS FOR SWING ABOARD AND DISC JOCKEYS

- Inform participants that landing on a disc may cause it to slide.

- Have group members agree to communicate their intentions when swinging towards the platform, discs or hoops. Have them plan together for the effect that a swinging body may have on a crowded area. Have participants agree to swing in a controlled manner.

- Agree not to allow participants on each other's shoulders at any time during this activity.

- Swing Aboard platforms and discs may be slippery if wet. Exercise caution and use additional spotters as needed.

- Have participants agree to ask for additional spotting if balance is precarious on the landing area.

PORTHOLE (HOLE IN ONE)

A large tire is suspended vertically between two supports at a height appropriate for the age and skill level of the participants. Tethers should be attached from eyes at the base of tire to eyes on support trees or poles to avoid excessive tire motion.

TASK
To have the entire group pass through the suspended tire. Once through the tire, a person cannot return to the beginning side of the tire to help (except to offer back-up spotting).

SPOTTING CONSIDERATIONS

- Consistent and effective spotting is required. Spotters must be alert to protecting the head, neck and shoulders throughout the tire pass.

- Warn spotters to watch for flailing arms and legs as a participant passes through the tire.

- Diving or jumping through the tire should not be allowed.

- Have spotters agree to bring participants carefully through the tire to avoid excessive rubbing of the tire on arms and legs.

FACILITATOR'S ROLE

- Be present on the far side of the tire to spot as needed as the first participant moves through the tire. Remain in that position until a sufficient numbers of participants have passed through the tire to handle spotting responsibilities. Similarly, move to the front side of the tire to spot the last person moving through the tire.

- Suggest and be supportive of a second attempt so that participants have the opportunity to build upon the lessons from their first experience.

- When working with younger audiences, consider using the guideline, "First person, feet first. Last person, head first." This statement helps to emphasize the importance of careful planning and attentive spotting.

VARIATIONS
Attempt to make the passage without touching the tire.

SEA GULL SWING TO THE SWINGING LOG

The Sea Gull Swing is a swing from a starting stump about 18" high to a landing platform which in this description is the Swinging Log. The swing rope should be attached high enough to provide a wide pendulum swing.

TASK

A participant, standing on the starting stump, attempts to swing to and land upon the Swinging Log without touching the ground.

SPOTTING CONSIDERATIONS

• It is important to emphasize that swingers not let go of the rope even if the swinger is directly over the landing area. Contact must be made with feet on the log and balance maintained before letting go of the rope.

• Clear communication must be used between the swinger and the spotters about her readiness to swing.

• Spotters at the landing perch need to be aware of the incoming swinger and should move in as necessary to prevent the swinger's shins and ankles from hitting the log. Further, if a swinger is not in a position to make a stable landing, spotters should be ready to move towards the swinger to lessen the swinging motion and bring her safely to a secure position.

• Spotters must continue to spot until a participant gains full balance and is safely on the ground.

• A swinger's knees should be flexed when trying to land on the platform.

FACILITATOR'S ROLE

• This is a very difficult event to spot. Therefore, there should be a prior assessment of the group's ability to competently spot dynamic motion.

• Demonstrate the correct path for the swing rope. To gain a sturdy landing spot on the Swinging Log, a participant must initiate a wide swinging arc from the stump to the log.

• Spotting positions and responsibilities should be thoroughly covered before beginning this activity.

• Safety on this event is predicated upon the swinger's ability to securely grip the rope. Prior experience with swinging elements such as the Nitro Crossing or Do I Go is recommended. Knowledge of a group's physical readiness for the Swing to the Swinging Log could be determined after observing participants during these events.

• There should be an awareness of each participant's ability to sustain a grip on the rope.

GROUP SIZE

10-20 participants. This element requires a number of carefully positioned spotters.

DEGREE OF DIFFICULTY

Advanced. Skills for spotting dynamic movement are needed.

SPIDER'S WEB

A prefabricated web strung between two trees, 10–14 feet apart, is comprised of approximately 15 to 17 open web sections. The web is constructed of Multi-line rope and bungee cord.

TASK

To pass each member of a group through a separate web opening, without letting any body part touch the web.

- Once a member has passed through an opening, that section of web is conceptually closed to further passage.

- Participants cannot be passed over or around the web.

SPOTTING CONSIDERATIONS

- Group members need to actively spot any participants who are lifted during their entire passage through the web.

- Participants should agree to never drop or let go of a participant because someone touched the web.

- As lifting may be required in this task, encourage participants to protect their backs by using their legs to lift.

- Do not allow diving or jumping through the web.

FACILITATOR'S ROLE

- Monitor the spotting and to be prepared to step in quickly if assistance is needed.

- Pay particular attention to the first and last participant through the web.

- It is recommended that participants be passed in a supine position (face up).

- When working with younger audiences, consider using the guideline, "First person, feet first. Last person, head first." This statement helps to emphasize the importance of careful planning and attentive spotting.

GROUP SIZE

For a single web, 8-12 people are ideal. If the web is L-shaped, the group can be larger. More holes, more action.

DEGREE OF DIFFICULTY

Intermediate.

VARIATIONS

There are many options and varying rules for the web. Some of the most popular are:

- If there are more people than spaces, allow two group members to go through the same hole before it is closed. Once chosen, these spaces cannot be changed.

- If anyone penetrates an opening in the web with any body part, that opening becomes exclusively hers to go through, regardless of the size of the opening.

- Modify the consequences for touching the web to match the ability of the participants. One option is to have the passed participant or even the group to begin again if a participant or a spotter on either side of the net touch the web.

- To weave an 11 mm climbing rope through the web. The rope must go through all holes of the web. The rope may not pass completely through the first hole until it passes through the last hole. Neither the rope nor any of the participants may touch any part of the web.

- Use spring-loaded clothespins to mark which web openings have already been used.

SWINGING LOG

The Swinging Log is most often represented by a 25-30 foot utility pole, suspended on cables between two trees approximately 10-12 inches off the ground. Swinging Logs should be tightly secured or detached when not in use to limit unsupervised access.

TASK

- One individual mounts and walks the length of the log, attempting to maintain her balance.

- **LOG PASS:** Two individuals mount the log on opposite ends. Their goal is to traverse the log bypassing each other in some fashion in the middle. Close spotting is required.

- **HIGH 5:** Two individuals attempt to meet in the center and give a High 5.

- **EXECUTIVE REACH:** From a distance of about two to three feet from the log (draw a line in the dirt), an individual attempts to step onto the log, gain balance and remain in place for five to ten seconds.

SPOTTING CONSIDERATIONS

- Be sure to demonstrate the potential movement of the log if a fall occurs. Spotters should be able to adjust their spotting positions to protect both themselves and the participant when a fall occurs. Emphasize that a sideways spotting stance will help to prevent shin injury.

- There are two spotting options. One is to designate a cluster of spotters, positioned on either side of the log, who will move alongside the traversing participant. A minimum of two spotters would be required in this method. A second option is to place spotters at intervals along each side of the log. Each spotter actively spots the participant as she passes. Good communication among spotters is necessary to insure that spotting is continuous throughout the traverse.

- Two people need to be in position at the ends of the log to grab the support cables to lessen the motion of the log after a participant falls or steps off. Rope tethers attached to the log could also be used to reduce log motion.

- Emphasize pro-active spotting; i.e., step toward, not away from.

- Spotters must never position themselves where they can be hit by the swinging log (including in between log and support trees).

GROUP SIZE

12-20 individuals. One or two individuals attempt the log as the remainder of the group spots.

DEGREE OF DIFFICULTY

Basic to Intermediate

- Have participants agree to not forcefully jump off the log, creating a wild swinging motion.

- Have participants agree not to run on the log.

FACILITATOR'S ROLE

- Give a complete demonstration of how the log can move and the various arcs through which it can swing.

- Alert the group to the log's mass and weight and potential for movement.

- Do not allow participants to sit on the log.

- As a facilitator, it may be a good practice to position yourself near the end cables of the log in the event that the spotter there needs assistance to slow/stop the motion of the log.

- On set-up and take-down of the log, make sure there are enough people to manage the weight of the log. Emphasize proper techniques for lifting.

VARIATIONS

- Walk the log backward or blindfolded.

- Swing to the Swinging Log. See Seagull Swing write-ups.

SWINGING TIRES

A series of tires are suspended from an overhead cable.

GROUP SIZE

8-12 participants. This activity can be time consuming for larger groups as the rotation of group members across the tires is slow.

TASK

The challenge is for the group to cross a designated area swinging from tire to tire. To enhance the teamwork aspect of the exercise, give the group a heavy object with a large handle that they must collectively transport from one side to the other.

DEGREE OF DIFFICULTY

Advanced.
This activity is strenuous and requires upper body strength.

SPOTTING CONSIDERATIONS

- Emphasize the importance of taking responsibility for self and recognizing personal limits. Participants should:

  - Dismount from the tires if they experience fatigue in the upper body (arms, shoulders, and hands).

  - Feel comfortable if a mid-traverse dismount is necessary.

  - Avoid getting a foot or other body part lodged inside the rim of a tire.

- Ask for spotting help if they become fatigued.

- Do not allow participants to swing with their heads below tire level.

- Spot participants as they are getting onto the first tire and off the last tire.

- Do not allow participants to swing in an uncontrolled manner on the tires.

FACILITATOR'S ROLE

- Check area underneath the tires for obstacles.

- Check tires to make sure they have open drain holes for water. If no drain holes have been drilled, empty the water by hand. Watch for squirrel nests/bee nests in the tires.

- Check to make sure that the eyebolts used to hang the tires are securely fastened.

VARIATIONS

To assist a group who may have members with less upper body strength, provide one or more intermediate resting platforms that would be situated out of the path of the swinging tires.

TEAM TROLLEY TRAVERSE

An adaptation of the Nitro Crossing element that allows for Universal Access. It features a 2' x 2' wooden platform suspended from a two wheel pulley system on an overhead cable. Prusik knots in the suspension system allow the platform's height to be easily adjusted. In this version, the trolley platform essentially fulfills the role of the Nitro swing rope.

TASK

For a group to cross the designated "river crossing" using only the trolley.

SPOTTING CONSIDERATIONS

• Only two participants should be on the trolley at any one time. Participants should ride in a sitting position.

• Encourage participants to push the trolley in a safe manner. Uncontrolled swinging of the apparatus should be avoided.

• Make sure spotters stay clear of the path of the trolley when it is moving on the cable.

• Spotters should assist in the loading and unloading of the platform.

FACILITATOR'S ROLE

Using the adjustable prusik system, set the trolley at an appropriate height for the age and skill level of the participants.

VARIATIONS

The Cannibal and Explorers Problem: Two groups of people are traveling together on a joint mission to find "the lost city of gold." There are an even number of each group, ie cannibals and explorers. They come to the "river" and all want to get across. The only means of transportation is a boat (trolley) that holds only two at a time. The explorers never want to be outnumbered by the cannibals, but they all must get across the river. As the boat is a row boat, at least one person must be in the trolley to cross. The cannibals can NEVER outnumber the explorers on either side of the "river". The problem is a logistical one in figuring out how to get everyone across.

GROUP SIZE

12-20 participants.

DEGREE OF DIFFICULTY

Basic.
A good introductory activity.

TP SHUFFLE

A utility pole or log, raised and supported in brackets a few inches off the ground.

TASK

A couple of options:

- Divide the group in half. Arrange the group so that each half is standing on opposite ends of the pole facing each other. The challenge is for each group to trade ends without anyone stepping off and touching the ground.

- Have the group line up categorically: for example, according to their birthdays in the calendar year.

SPOTTING CONSIDERATIONS

- Agree that if a participant steps or falls off the log, she will step to the ground and try to not pull off anyone else.

- Spot as needed particularly if two participants are having difficulty attempting a pass.

VARIATIONS

- Add a time limit and assign penalty seconds for anyone who falls off.

- Start the problem where each group moves backward and ends up backward.

- Do the activity non-verbally.

- Place a hula hoop on the ground that can be used as a free space by any member of the group.

GROUP SIZE

8-14 participants

DEGREE OF DIFFICULTY

Basic.
Good beginning activity to get group comfortable with appropriate touch and spotting.

TRIANGLE TENSION TRAVERSE

This element is formed by a triangle of tightly strung cables approximately 2 to 2½ feet above the ground. Three lengths of Multi-line rope are attached to each of the three trees. These lines provide some support as participants attempt to walk along the cable.

TASK

For an individual to attempt to traverse around the cables using the suspended ropes. Three participants may go at the same time if there are enough spotters.

SPOTTING CONSIDERATIONS

- Spotters need to be aware of the nature of a fall from the Tension Traverse. A falling participant will tend to fall back towards the starting point, particularly if they maintain contact with the rope. To be effective, spotters need to position themselves accordingly, one half step back toward the starting point.

- A minimum of two spotters is required, one in front and one in back. If the terrain is more difficult, additional spotters should be used.

- Falls happen quickly on this event. Spotters need to maintain a ready position at all times. If a fall occurs, spotters should move in to support the participant.

- Spotters need to move laterally with the traversing participant.

- Spotters need to be aware of the possibility of a participant's flailing arms as she tries to maintain a balanced position.

- Participants should be advised to help themselves by stepping down from the cable if a fall is imminent and unavoidable.

- Rapid traversing movement on the cable should be discouraged.

VARIATIONS

- Move out and back on the cable. The return is often more difficult.

- A participant tries to complete the triangle, moving out one cable, across the back, and forward on the last triangle leg using just one of the Multi-line ropes. Spotting must occur on all legs. Realize that a participant will be leaning backwards on the back cable.

GROUP SIZE

12-15 individuals.
Each participant on the cables must be spotted by a minimum of two spotters.

DEGREE OF DIFFICULTY

Basic to Intermediate.
Attentive spotting skills
are required.

TROLLEYS

Trolleys are usually represented by two sturdy 4 x 4's that are no more than 12 feet in length. Five-foot ropes, spaced at 12-inch intervals, provide hand-lines for participants.

TASK

- To have a group move along a prescribed route. This is usually done by having participants place right feet on one of the 4 x 4's and left feet on the other. Participants may hold their respective ropes for balance.

- If a participant falls off during an attempt, one option is to have the group return to the starting point to begin again.

- Allow the students to figure out how to use the Trolleys. Don't give the solution when you present the activity.

SPOTTING CONSIDERATIONS

Encourage participants to step off the Trolleys if they are losing their balance to avoid a group tumble.

FACILITATOR'S ROLE

- Check the area for obstacles— crossing uneven ground can snap the trolley boards.

- Check to make sure that the trolley hand lines are securely connected to the boards.

VARIATIONS

- If a participant falls off the trolleys, that individual is allowed to remount, but must be facing in the opposite direction or become blindfolded.

- Alternatively, if a participant falls off, she must move to the front of the line and become the lead person; i.e., the person most apt to fall prey to the domino syndrome.

- For more activity, use shorter trolley lengths sized to accommodate 4-6 people. These shorter lengths may be constructed so that they can be connected together with rapid links. Additional links may add to the difficulty.

- Create an obstacle course with various tasks for the group to complete along the way. These challenges could metaphorically stand for goals and responsibilities of the group.

GROUP SIZE

Limited only by the number of available positions on the trolley.

DEGREE OF DIFFICULTY

Basic.
A good introductory group exercise.

TRUST FALL

Suitable areas for the Trust Fall activity include platforms, stumps or a series of graduated steps. The steps for bleachers found in sport settings are also appropriate.

TASK
For a participant to perform a controlled fall into the arms of spotters.

SPOTTING CONSIDERATIONS

SPOTTERS:
• The group is arranged in two parallel lines facing each other.

• Arms are zippered, extended and bent at the elbows, palms facing up.

• Feet are in stride position. Foot farthest from the platform and the faller is extended forward.

• Knees are flexed. Giving with the knees slightly on a catch provides for a softer landing.

• Spotters are positioned shoulder to shoulder (Velcro shoulders) to ensure a strong and tight catching bed of arms.

• Spotters' heads are comfortably back.

• Spotters should have a clear understanding of the strongest and most appropriate position to catch the faller.

• Full attention is focused on the faller at all times.

• Spotters should be positioned close enough to the Trust Fall platform to close up any open space in the event that a faller sits or "folds".

• Upon catching a faller, spotters need to pay close attention to the faller until she is in an upright, standing position on the ground. If needed, the spotters should assist the faller to that position.

• Clear communication between the spotters and the faller needs to happen on every attempt. For example,

Faller:	**"Spotter's ready?"**
Spotters:	**"Ready to Catch (insert name)"**
Faller:	**"Falling"**
Spotters:	**"Fall"**

GROUP SIZE

A minimum of eight catchers (spotters) is required.

DEGREE OF DIFFICULTY

Advanced.
The spotting skills of a group must be reliable. A group should be working well together and have built a solid level of trust.

FALLERS:

- Fallers should maintain a rigid position with head slightly back for the fall. Fallers should try to avoid a sitting position as it makes for a more difficult catch.

- Hands and arms should be fixed in an interlocking system or other suitable technique that would prevent arms from flailing and injuring spotters.

- At the direction of a designated spotter, a faller is positioned so that her fall will be straight into the arms of the waiting spotters.

- After falling and being caught, fallers should ask spotters to assist them to a vertical standing position.

FACILITATOR'S ROLE

- It is important to emphasize participation by choice in this activity due to the trust fall's inherent physical and emotional challenges.

- A maximum height for Trust Falls is 5 feet. However, an appropriate height could be lower as it is dependent upon the size, age and skill of the group.

- The facilitator should never be the first person to fall.

- Be sure the group goes through a series of warm-up exercises and/or trust sequence before leading into this activity.

- Only attempt this activity when a group appears ready, motivated and demonstrating trustworthy behavior.

- Depending upon the height and configuration of the trust fall platform, a participant might be designated to spot the faller as she readies for the fall.

- Make sure all jewelry, watches, pencils and pens are removed from all fallers. It is recommended that spotters remove base-ball caps or turn them backwards.

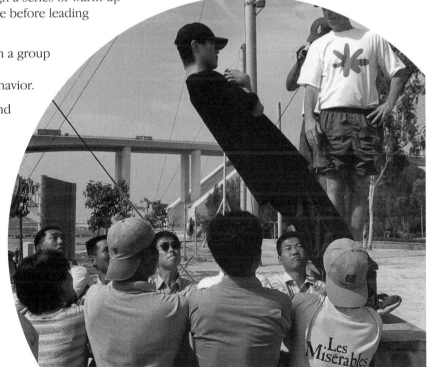

TRUST DIVE:

This activity is often considered to be a lead-up activity before the Hickory Jump (a low element) and ultimately the Pamper Pole or Plank. Trust dives are generally made from heights a bit lower than those used for Trust Falls.

THE TRUST DIVE DIFFERS FROM THE TRUST FALL IN THE FOLLOWING WAYS:

• Each person in the double-flanking spotting line takes a quarter turn toward the diver. Considering the forward momentum of the diver, this position better prepares the group for the catch.

• The first two catchers in the spotting lines should be 2-3 feet away from the edge of the bleachers (or platform) or at a distance that makes the diver comfortable.

• The diver must dive straight out toward an invisible goal, not down into the group. The diver should dive with hands in front and over-head, as if diving into a pool, keeping arms in front for the landing.

• The diver must remove any type of metal adornment that might cause injury to the catchers such as western belt buckles etc.

• The group can use the same set of commands that were used during the Trust Fall.

THE WALL

A smooth-surfaced wall, usually 12 feet in height, is secured to four 4' x 4' horizontal cross-supports. The 4 x 4 supports are bolted to two utility poles or two conveniently spaced trees. Many walls feature a small platform on the upper backside of The Wall. This serves as a secure base for spotters positioned at the top of The Wall. Descent down the backside of The Wall can be by ladder or horizontally placed staples in one of the support trees.

TASK

- Using all members, the group must get everyone up and over The Wall starting on the smooth-surfaced side.

- The group may have a maximum of three persons on the top of The Wall, assisting a fourth person up and over. (The maximum number of spotters can vary according to the size of the platform behind The Wall. Realize that too many people may cause confusion.)

- The sides of The Wall and support poles cannot be used.

- Articles of clothing may not be used as props.

SPOTTING CONSIDERATIONS

- Participants should agree to support everyone's effort.

- Allow only a maximum of three people on top of The Wall at one time and one in transition. (See introductory description)

- Have an appropriate number of spotters on the front and back of The Wall at all times with their focus on spotting.

- Have spotters form a half-circle or "cocoon of spotters" around the person being lifted up The Wall. Explain to the group that falls can happen in any direction, away from The Wall as well as laterally to either side.

- Have participants agree that, when standing on the doubled 4 x 4's or platform at the top of The Wall, both feet will be planted firmly at all times.

- Have participants agree not to hang an individual by the legs in order to reach the last member of the group.

- Have participants use the staples or ladder when descending down the back. NO JUMPING! A spotter should be on hand to assist the descent.

GROUP SIZE

A group must be large enough to have an adequate number of available spotters at all times.

DEGREE OF DIFFICULTY

Advanced.

- Encourage spotters to maintain clear communication throughout the exercise so that only one person at a time is either ascending the front of The Wall or descending the backside of The Wall.

- Make sure all jewelry, watches, pencils and pens are removed from all participants.

- Once a person has gone over The Wall, they become spotters only. They can no longer assist someone going over The Wall.

FACILITATOR'S ROLE

- Inspect poles and support braces for soundness.

- Do not allow participants to insert their fingers in the cracks between the boards or in an available knothole.

- Make sure that the top and face of The Wall are smooth and free of splinters.

- Make sure that no nails are protruding from The Wall.

- Review spotting procedures, and remind the group of the importance of group spotting due to the height of the obstacle. Talk about the difficulty of trying to catch a falling participant from the top of The Wall.

- Pay particular attention to spotting the backside of The Wall.

- Stress the importance of spotting an individual throughout the entire task.

- Stress proper lifting and support, especially when participants are standing on other participants' shoulders or are being lifted up to that position.

- Do not allow the group to use belts, shoelaces or other articles of clothing as aids to get over The Wall.

- Do not allow a participant's head to be in a position where it is below her feet.

VARIATIONS

- For a group that may have difficulty with the height of The Wall, a suitably-strong rope can be attached to the top of The Wall and flipped over to the front. A hole is often drilled in the top 4' x 4' for this purpose. Make sure that the rope placement has been approved and inspected by a professional vendor.

- Invite the group to set a goal as to how many participants they would like to see get up and over The Wall. All members of the group would then not have to be passed over The Wall.

- Attempt the task non-verbally.

WHALE WATCH

The Whale Watch is generally built as an approximately 8' x 12' wooden platform balanced on a 6' x 6' fulcrum beam.

TASK
To have the group execute a challenge or a series of challenges utilizing the teetering deck of the Whale Watch. See variations.

SPOTTING CONSIDERATIONS
- Encourage participants to watch out for each other while on the Whale Watch especially to avoid any misstep off the platform.

- Indicate that no one at any time should allow any body part, especially fingers and toes, to slip beneath the ends of the platform. Emphasize that the platform is heavy and moves up and down with momentum.

FACILITATOR'S ROLE
- Present the various scenarios succinctly and clearly.

- When a group is exiting from the Whale Watch, encourage the group to depart from the same end to prevent anyone from suddenly getting flipped off the high end. There should be no jumping off the sides.

- The Whale Watch platform should not be used as a macro teeter-totter.

- Whale Watch platforms vary in size and configuration and hence may have different weight limits. Exercise caution to not overload the platform.

VARIATIONS
- With all participants aboard and in balance, have group members rotate positions. Possibilities are circle shuffles and side-to-side exchanges.

- A group begins on the ground. The challenge is to load all group members onto the Whale Watch, entering from the two ends. A variety of different consequences can be introduced if an end of the Whale Watch touches the ground.

GROUP SIZE

Ideally 12 participants, but upwards of 20 can participate, albeit a crowd.

DEGREE OF DIFFICULTY

Basic to Intermediate. Challenge levels vary depending upon the presented task.

- A crossing of the Whale Watch can be attempted, with all members starting on the ground at one end of the platform. Only one touch is allowed.

- Place a small beach ball on the Whale Watch platform amidst the feet of all participants. Attempt to have everyone exit from the Whale Watch while keeping the beach ball in balance on the platform. The beach ball may not be held in place by feet or hands.

- Squares may be inscribed on the Whale Watch. A game of Checkers can be played. Two teams situated on either end of the Whale Watch facing each other take turns making moves as in a Checkers game. If a team causes the Whale Watch to hit the ground, the turn goes to the other team.

WILD WOOSEY

Two tautly strung cables diverging from approximately the same point, connect with two distant anchors that are located about 14 feet apart. This creates a "V". Both cables are no more than 16 inches above the ground.

TASK

TWO OPTIONS:

- For two participants—one per cable— to walk the angled cables maintaining constant physical contact with one another. They go to the point where they can no longer continue (they break contact) or until they reach the far support trees.

- Present this as a group problem, not for individual pairs. (See variations)

SPOTTING CONSIDERATIONS

- Understand that participants can fall in any direction when first mounting the cable.

- Spotters located outside the cables are most important for the first 10-15 feet of the activity.

- *Do not allow* participants to interlock fingers while attempting the activity.

THERE ARE TWO DIFFERENT TECHNIQUES USED FOR SPOTTING POTENTIAL INWARD FALLS ON THE WILD WOOSEY.

GUIDELINES FOR THE FIRST ARE AS FOLLOWS:

- Spotters assume a waist-bent position directly beneath the on-cable participants. Spotters' hands are placed on top of their knees to provide back support.

- Spotters should move only as fast as the participants, staying beneath the cable walkers.

- As the two participants maneuver farther apart on the cables, more spotters should be added beneath the cable walkers.

GROUP SIZE

Two on-cable participants with a team of spotters: two spotters each on the outside of the cables plus additional spotters beneath the traversing pair.
The spotters in the center will increase in number as the duo progresses outward from the starting point.

DEGREE OF DIFFICULTY

Basic.

GUIDELINES FOR THE SECOND TECHNIQUE ARE:

• Have spotters align themselves as in the trust fall (two parallel zippered lines of two or more spotters each. Number of spotters depends upon width of cables.). This group then moves underneath the cable duo keeping pace with their progress. Some spotters will be stepping backwards and others moving forward. Falls are caught in the zipper. Participants must be helped back to a standing position.

FACILITATOR'S ROLE

Be aware of potential injuries from this event: finger injuries from interlocking hands, uncomfortable pain from undue pressure on wrists, back injury from unsupported backs while spotting underneath the cable walkers.

VARIATIONS

• Establish a point on the cables that participants will attempt to reach and then return from to the start. If pairs make it to end, attempt a return to the beginning.

• Create a group problem: add together the distance traversed by each pair to create a group goal.

THE HIGH CHALLENGE COURSE

Mention the words "Challenge Course" and often images of high-wire balancing elements, "leaps of faith", and exhilarating rides down speedy Zip Wires come to mind. Although it is true that there is a myriad of innovative and exciting High Challenge Course events, many adventure practitioners today view the high elements as the culminating point in a group's experience in which to refine, test, and celebrate the skills, trust and cohesiveness of a group. The high challenge experience serves as the pinnacle of a journey that begins simply with get-to-know-you activities and progresses through a sequence of increasingly more difficult exercises. Its value and purpose far outreach momentary rushes of adrenaline. In a well-sequenced program that offers opportunities for reflection, participants may have experiences that open new ways of thinking about themselves or other members of the group. The high elements often provide the catalyst that stretch participants to the edge of their comfort zone to a place where personal breakthroughs and the opportunities for change are found.

Types of Challenge Courses

It is believed that the first challenge course was built at the Colorado Outward Bound School (COBS) in 1961/1962 (Herb Kincey). Today, there are more than 6000 Challenge Courses in the United States. Although these courses vary in many ways such as the diversity of populations served and the types of elements offered, most can be categorized by either of two styles of belay: static or dynamic. Many of the earliest courses were static or circuit courses. Static courses feature a journey-style experience offering the climber a series of continuous interconnected elements. Protection for the climber is usually provided by a short adjustable lanyard equipped with two separate tethers that link the climber's harness to an overhead belay cable. Participants are monitored by instructors positioned on high transfer platforms typically located at the start or end point of each different element. The other type of belay system features a dynamic belay. With this set-up, a climber usually undertakes only one element at a time. Each climber is connected to a rope that runs directly from her harness through an overhead belay set-up and back to a designated belayer on the ground whose primary job is to manage the appropriate tension of the climber's rope throughout the climb. The climber in this system can be easily lowered to the ground at any point during the climb.

Setting Up the Challenge Course

EQUIPMENT FOR BELAY SET-UP

Over the years, there has been a steady evolution in the design of belay set-up hardware. Initial systems often featured two side by side steel carabiners or rapid links on the belay cable. Whereas this set-up is still acceptable according to ACCT standards, improved technology has seen increased use of pulleys and shear reduction devices to respectively facilitate the movement of hardware along the belay cable and to reduce rope shear. All equipment used in the belay set-up must have a minimum tensile strength of 5000 lbs.

Cable pulley with rapid link and shear reduction device for use on traversing element

Shear reduction device with rapid link for non-traversing element

CABLE PULLEYS

Pulleys used in challenge course set-ups are strong stainless steel pulleys with steel sheaves designed for use on cable. They often feature tensile strengths over 12,000 lbs. They are used most frequently on traversing elements to facilitate movement of the belay set-up.

RAPID LINKS

Rapid links are commonly used as connectors on a challenge course in applications that range from the attachment of swing ropes to the connection of belay hardware. Zinc coated twelve and fourteen millimeter rapid links are the most commonly used sizes as they often feature tensile strengths of 16,500 lbs. and 24,200 lbs. respectively. In belay set-ups, the orientation of the rapid link is important. The link should be positioned so that the screw gate tightens in a downward motion to offset the chance of cable vibration working open a gate. Gravity will help to maintain the closed position. Rapid links must also be completely tightened so that no threads are visible. A partially closed rapid link will be less strong and will deform under considerable pressure. Recommended is the French brand, Maillon-Rapide, which is considered to be one of the highest quality links.

SHEAR REDUCTION DEVICES

ACCT standard B7.1 requires that belay ropes on dynamic belay systems turn over a fitting with a minimum diameter of 12 mm or .47". This standard is designed to reduce the amount of shear or stress to a rope and to increase its life span. Shear reduction devices used in belay set-ups often exceed the ACCT standard further reducing shear and thereby helping to maintain the original breaking strength of the rope.

At High 5, we commonly install several different types of belay set-ups. See photos to left and right.

Cable pulley with two steel carabiners for use on traversing element

Two steel carabiners on cable

**Loop
on end
of belay rope**

SET-UP METHODS FOR HIGH ELEMENTS

Challenge course instructors have several options for setting up high elements. Each of the methods has its advantages and disadvantages and requires different skill levels. At no time should an instructor attempt to exceed her level of skill and ability in this area.

The methods are as follows:

- Pulling the belay rope up with a haul cord
- Accessing the belay cable using a self-belay system (Lobster Claws with Zorbers) for fall protection
- Accessing the belay cable using a cable grab system that provides fall protection system for the climber.
- Accessing the belay cable using a traditional belay system. This method requires two people.

HAUL CORDS

A haul cord (also called #4 nylon cord, parachute cord, or Lazy Line) is secured onto the end of the belay rope. Once attached, a belay rope can be pulled up and through the overhead shear reduction device. The procedure is reversed to remove the belay rope.

The advantage to this type of system is that it allows a quick and easy set up of climbing ropes. This may be great time-saver for courses that are used frequently or ones that need to be run on tight schedules.

There are also disadvantages to haul cords. Sometimes, they can get stuck and fail to move smoothly especially in softwood trees with sap. Also, they frequently get pulled down. Usually, this happens either because the climbing rope/haul cord connection is not secure or there's a failure to hold onto the end of the haul cord, especially in taking down climbing ropes. The weight of the climbing rope on its descent will cause the lighter haul rope to whip out of a participant's hand if not held tightly.

Another disadvantage to haul cords is that facilitators do not have to climb to set up the belay system. Ironic as this may seem, climbing on a regular basis on your course does achieve two important objectives. First, it helps to maintain your climbing and self-belay skills as well as a familiarity with your course. Secondly, and more significantly, it helps to ensure that your belay set-ups are properly installed. It is critical that all belay set-ups be checked before each use.

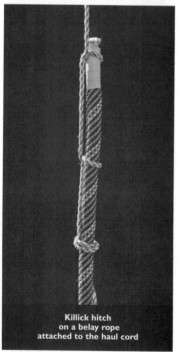

**Killick hitch
on a belay rope
attached to the haul cord**

USE OF SELF-BELAY SYSTEMS

Self-belay systems allow facilitators climbing access to their courses without a traditional belay. Protection for the climber is provided by a lanyard (also often called a lobster claw) that has two specific tethers radiating from a central core. The end of each tether is equipped with either a steel clip or steel carabiner. A facilitator climbs with the lanyard by alternately clipping each individual tether into appropriate protection points during the ascent. In a rhythmic fashion, a climber continuously removes the lower of the two clipped tethers and re-clips it to a new higher protection point. It is important to clip as high and often as possible. The tethers of the self-belay device should always be clipped into points that are at waist height or higher. This is to prevent a long and potentially painful fall. Further, a facilitator should only clip into protection points that are designed to bear the weight of a fall. Upon reaching the belay cable, the climber can adjust the self-belay by using a variety of clip-in techniques to establish a safe and comfortable working stance. The self belay system should only be used by climbers who have received training with this technique and who feel comfortable at height.

Self-belay lanyards have evolved in recent years to reflect updated standards related to leading edge climbing. Section C8 of ACCT's Challenge Course Standards describe the following specifications for personal fall arrest systems. "Personal fall arrest systems shall limit the maximum arresting force on the person to 900 lbs. (4.0 kn) when used with a seat harness and limit the free fall distance to no more than 6' (183 cm.). To comply with this standard, lanyards should now be equipped with a load-limiting device which will reduce the impact from a fall. Zorbers, an example of a load-limiting device, activates when forces reach 450 lbs. At this point, its sewn tear-stitch webbing gradually releases.

ACCEPTABLE SELF-BELAY ANCHOR POINTS

If you are going to be doing self-belayed climbing on your course, it is important to review with your challenge course vendor as to which anchor points are acceptable clip-in points with a self-belay lanyard. Installation practices vary. Your builder will be able to provide input as to the strength and reliability of the materials on your course. Hardware testing in recent years has shifted ACCT standards, particularly in regards to the suitability of some clip-in points such as staples. Staples are generally not recommended as clip-in points. Lead anchor bolts supported by 5/8" lag screws or other alternative methods described further in the text now serve as other access options. It is always wise to be conservative when climbing on self-belays to clip into reliable protection points.

Lead anchor bolt

The following table briefly outlines generally acceptable and not acceptable self-belay anchor points. As previously stated, it is wise to always first consult with your challenge course installer.[1]

ACCEPTABLE SELF-BELAY ANCHOR POINTS	NOT ACCEPTABLE SELF-BELAY ANCHOR POINTS
Forged nut eyebolts (5/8" or larger)	Hand ropes or cables (Burma Bridge)
Belay cables (backed up)	Burma Bridge Cross Arm Braces
Belay cable back-up loops	Strandvise bails
Cables supporting Cat Walk log	Shoulder lag eye screws
Forged shoulder lag eye screws (5/8")	Cables that are not backed up
Lead Anchor bolts (with 5/8" lag screws)	Wooden Platforms in trees
Swaged or cable clamp loops that are attached to through bolts	Small 3/8" staples
Rapid links attached to through bolts	Loop between cable clamp and serving sleeve

Cable Grab Device

CABLE GRAB SYSTEMS

Cable grab systems provide another method of fall protection for the climber. Featured in this system is a mechanical cable grab device that attaches to a vertical cable installed on the tree or pole of a climbing element. A camming mechanism in this device allows it free movement up or down the cable except when subjected to strong downward motions. Such forces on the device lock it firmly onto the cable. To use, a climber attaches the cable grab to her harness with a short secure tether. She then can ascend or descend a stapled tree or pole by moving the cable grab upwards or downwards in correspondence with her climbing motions.

ACCESS VIA A DYNAMIC BELAY (TWO PEOPLE)

A simple and inexpensive method for accessing belay cables is to install a separate belay point at the top of a climb on the access tree. With the use of a haul cord, a traditional dynamic belay can then be easily set-up. A climber on belay is then protected to climb to set up or retrieve belay gear. A second person who serves as the belayer is required in this method.

| Adapted from information in The Guide for Challenge Course Operations by Bob Ryan 2005

Equipment for the High Challenge Course

There is a wide array of equipment available to the Challenge Course practitioner. Harnesses, carabiners, ropes, and helmets vary in color, style, fit, and price. Your final choice may ultimately depend upon your budget and personal preference, but should also reflect your program goals and objectives. Following is some information and guidelines to aid in that equipment decision-making process.

ROPE

11mm (millimeter) nylon climbing rope is the rope of choice for most dynamically-belayed challenge courses. Durable, easy to handle and with tensile strengths over 5000 lbs, this workhorse of the rope world is suitable for the high participant volumes typical of most challenge courses. Most common are dynamic ropes that feature some stretch and are designed to absorb the impact and shock from falls. Static ropes that have less stretch than dynamic ropes are traditionally used for rappelling and rescue situations. However, static ropes may be used as belay ropes in particular applications where less stretch is desired. The Flying Squirrel element is one example where a low elongation rope is preferable.

ROPE CARE

Rope has a limited shelf life. It varies from one rope manufacturer to another, but in general, according to the Cordage Institute is no longer than seven years. The actual length of a rope's life however is dependent upon several factors such as frequency of use, care received, age, and type of usage. Ropes should be inspected each time they are used for cuts, frays, excessive fuzziness, and unusual lumpiness. If any of these conditions are found, ropes should be immediately set aside for review by a professional challenge course inspector or retired permanently. Professional inspections of all challenge course equipment should be scheduled annually.

NMG Xiamen, China 2002

- Ropes should be properly stored between periods of use. Ropes should be neatly coiled or stowed in secure storerooms or bins that will not get excessively hot. Ropes should not be left on unpainted concrete floors as base chemicals may leach into rope fibers.

- Knots should always be removed from the rope after use. This helps to ensure a more even wear in the rope ends. Further, and as importantly, it promotes knot tying practice.

- Ropes should be cleaned periodically. Ropes can be easily washed in an automatic front-loading machine using warm water and a small amount of mild soap or detergent. Top-loading washers may cause rope damage. Ropes should be thoroughly line dried before coiling.

- Ropes should be stored away from contaminants such as acids, bleaching compounds, and unknown chemicals. Also, be aware that the insect repellent DEET may degrade rope.

- Avoid stepping on rope. Dirt from the ground or bottoms of shoes can be ground into the rope working like tiny knives to abrade the rope's fibers. A dirty rope will also cause extra wear on belay devices.

- Use belay ropes only for climbing. Do not use them as game boundary markers, jump ropes, or tug of war. Retired ropes can serve this purpose.

- Do periodic maintenance on belay ropes. Repair frayed ends.

- Ropes should be taken down from a course after each use. This makes sense not only for security reasons but it also keeps the ropes from excessive UV exposure.

ROPE LOGS

It is a good idea to keep a rope log that records the date of purchase, days of use, and the number of climbs for each individual rope on a challenge course. Ropes can be separately identified by a variety of systems: color coding, naming the rope etc. Rope logs provide useful information for the Challenge Course manager particularly in determining how often she will have to purchase new ropes for specific elements. As well, it gives the Challenge Course inspector a detailed history of each rope used on a course.

HARNESSES

Commercial harnesses have become the norm in recent years for most challenge course programs. Convenience, comfort, and simplicity are reasons most often cited for this preference. Tied harnesses such as Swiss seats or Studebaker wraps however are still used in some programs. Although these systems are now less popular, their use is often directly based on specific goals for their adventure program. How might those goals influence the choice of harness? To answer that question, the following criteria may be useful:

TIED SEAT HARNESSES
(SWISS SEATS OR STUDEBAKER WRAPS)

PROS

- **COST.** Swiss seats and Studebaker Wraps are usually created from lengths of 9 mm kernmantle rope. This material is durable, strong, and relatively inexpensive.

- **SKILL DEVELOPMENT.** Tying your own harness creates a sense of ownership and responsibility. Participants feel a sense of pride and accomplishment in mastering this skill.

- **INSPECTION.** Tied harnesses can be easily inspected for wear and proper fit.

- **MAINTENANCE.** With proper care, rope harnesses need little maintenance.

- **ADAPTABILITY.** Studebaker wraps can be cut to different lengths and thus can be easily adapted to a variety of body sizes. Also, clipping a belay rope into the back of a Studebaker wrap for trapeze events is acceptable.

CONS

- Needs periodic adjustment and tightening.

- Is less comfortable, particularly on trapeze-type events.

- Takes more time to teach and a higher skill level to put on properly.

- Requires more time to put on.

Tied seat harness

**Commercial
Seat Harness
Front**

**Commercial
Seat Harness
Rear**

COMMERCIAL SEAT HARNESSES

PROS

- **COMFORT.** The waistband and leg loops in commercial harnesses are usually constructed of wide seat-belt webbing which generally adds comfort. In more expensive harnesses, these segments are often padded. Comfort might be important in the following situations: working with older populations or people with disabilities, rock climbing trips, or for facilitators who spend time in the trees setting up climbs.

- **SIMPLICITY.** Commercial harnesses generally are quick and easy to put on. They require less overall instruction.

- **ACCEPTANCE.** Participants like them. There is usually less resistance to wearing a commercial harness.

CONS

- **EXPENSE.** For programs with lots of students, harness costs add up quickly.

- **ADAPTABILITY.** Very few harnesses are specifically designed for challenge course use and only a few allow for clipping the belay into the back of the harness for trapeze-type events. Harnesses must always be used according to the manufacturer's recommendations. For example, one could not clip into the back of a harness that was not designed for that purpose.

- **HARDER TO INSPECT.** Commercial harnesses need to be visually inspected for wear and abrasion, integrity of the buckling system, and soundness of stitching.

- **FIT.** Some harnesses are said to be "universal" in that one size fits all. This may be the case in most instances, but may not provide the best fit for smaller or larger individuals. In these cases, other harness alternatives may be necessary. Proper fit is critical. Things to watch for are: does the harness sit above the hipbones; does it fit snugly on the torso? Is there at least 3 inches of "tail" left over after the waistband buckle has been properly secured?

CHEST HARNESSES

USES. Chest harnesses are used on a challenge course for a variety of different reasons. Some of the most common are:

- To help maintain an upright body position. Individuals with a large percentage of their weight located in their upper bodies often struggle to maintain a vertical position when hanging on a rope if wearing just a seat harness. A chest harness properly fitted and connected to a seat harness will usually provide a higher clip-in point thus raising one's center of gravity and hence adding stability.

- Comfort. A chest harness with a seat harness provides additional support for the body. Individuals requiring extra support such as people with bad backs may benefit from this type of system. Full body harnesses are another option for these participants.

- For use on elements that offer a back clip-in option for the belay. The chest harness in combination with the seat harness provides a more upright posture as well as greater stability on these elements. Also, on Pamper Pole and Flying Squirrel events, the back-clipped belay rope is away from the face and arms of the participant reducing the likelihood of rope contact.

Rear clip-in
to seat and
chest harness

FIT. Chest harnesses like seat harnesses must be used according to the manufacturer's instructions. Most are designed for just a front clip belay. A few feature the option of both a front and/or back-clip. It is critical that the chest harness be properly fitted in either of these situations. A poorly fitted chest harness could actually cause more harm than not wearing one at all. Professional training is recommended to learn this skill.

HELMETS

Helmets are now required climbing equipment on challenge courses. In the past, helmets had been mandatory on some elements but not on others. To eliminate the confusion and to align with the widespread norm of helmet use as personal safety equipment, helmets have become an accepted practice. As with all equipment, it is important that helmets fit properly. This means a fit that is snug enough to prevent side to side or front to back wobble. Younger participants with smaller heads often have a difficult time being correctly sized in a helmet. Helmets that feature adjustable head bands or are designed for younger populations are good choices.

CARABINERS

Carabiners are a versatile and indispensable piece of equipment on a challenge course. Light, strong with tensile strengths over 5000 lbs and easy to use, these clips come in a variety of shapes, sizes, materials, and operating styles. The choice of carabiner is most often determined by type of usage.

USES OF LOCKING, NON-LOCKING, AND AUTO-LOCK CARABINERS

STANDARD LOCKING CARABINERS are to be used in all belay applications. They may also be used to attach a self-belay lanyard to a seat harness and to connect a zip tether to a climber's harness.

NON-LOCKING CARABINERS may only be used in non-belay situations such as attaching swing ropes or setting up low elements like the Maze or Spider's Web.

SINGLE STAGE AUTO-LOCKING CARABINERS or Twist-locks should not be used in belay situations. Auto-lock gate openings have been reported when contact with a foot cable, staple or rope has rubbed across their gates. There are two applications on a challenge course however where they are commonly used. On Zip Wire tethers, auto locking carabiners are often used to connect the zip lanyard directly to the zip pulley. An auto lock is preferable here as it will remain closed as the zip pulley runs along the cable. A standard locking carabiner may loosen and open from the vibrations of the moving pulley. Also, steel single stage auto locks are sometimes used on the ends of self-belay tethers.

TWO STAGE AUTO LOCKING CARABINERS have become popular in recent years. Designed with a twist and slide gate mechanism, these carabiners require two separate steps to open and close them. They are suitable for belay applications.

STEEL VERSUS ALUMINUM CARABINERS

Steel carabiners are heavier, but more durable than aluminum alloy carabiners. Steel carabiners can be attached directly to a belay cable as they resist wear better than an aluminum carabiner. Thus, steel carabiners are preferred in rescue belay set-ups.

Aluminum carabiners are lighter than steel. They are used most often for belay attachments. Because of the softness of the material, they are not recommended for direct use on a belay cable.

All carabiners need to be visually inspected on a regular basis for excessive wear and for proper operation of the gate. If an aluminum carabiner is dropped from height, it may sustain stress fractures. As these fractures cannot be seen without the aid of an X-ray, it is generally prudent to retire the piece.

BELAY DEVICES

Belay devices are designed to increase friction in a belay system giving greater holding power. Friction in belay devices is caused by having rope pass through a restricted opening and then bending it around a post (usually a carabiner fixed to a harness). There currently are many different belay devices available today. Most are aperture-style devices such as slots (Sticht plates) and tubes (Tubers, Pyramids, ATCs) through which a bight of rope is pushed and secured to a locking carabiner on the harness. Figure-8 devices have also been used, although they are less common now. Figure eights however were originally designed for rappelling, not belaying. Figure-eights that are to be used for belaying should be approved by the manufacturer for that purpose.

There also are camming belay devices in the marketplace. This piece of equipment is designed to automatically jam and lock off the rope in the event of a fall. As fail-safe as this feature sounds, camming devices require proper training. Lowering climbers properly with this type of belay device takes skill and practice. Camming devices such as Gri-Gri's are also expensive relative to other belay devices.

Choosing a belay device is a decision reflecting personal preference. One will find a variance in the different styles in the amount of friction created, handling smoothness, and heat generation caused by friction. Be aware that Figure-eights add twist to the rope which after time can result in spaghetti-like piles of cordage.

RESCUE BAGS

A fully stocked Challenge Course Rescue Bag should be on site at a challenge course whenever any climbing is to occur. It is a good policy to leave the Rescue Bag in the same spot each time, a place known to instructors and of easy access to them. The contents of the bag should be made off limits to participants. It is also a good practice to take an inventory of this equipment prior to every climbing program.

The contents of a rescue bag for a standard one or two person cutaway rescue using the prusik sling technique is as follows:

1 11 mm static kernmantle rope cut long enough to set up a belay on your highest element

1 Harness for the rescuer

1 Self-belay lanyard with clips

4 Locking carabiners

2 Steel locking carabiners

1-2 Figure eight descenders

1-2 Belay device(s)

3-4 7' 5.5mm spectra cord slings

1 Pair trauma scissors

1 Pair belay gloves

1 Cable pulley (optional)

Rescue bag contents are best stowed in a portable daypack.

Body
Belay

The Belay

The high elements on a challenge course require a method of participant protection known as a belay system. The belay system uses rope, carabiners and other specialized hardware to provide protection for anyone climbing higher than can be safely spotted from the ground.

TYPES OF BELAY

On a typical High 5 Challenge Course, four possible belay systems might be used: a dynamic belay, a modification of the dynamic belay called an Australian belay, a static belay and a self-belay.

IN A DYNAMIC BELAY, a designated person, the belayer, is responsible for managing the safety of the climber. She does this through the use of applied friction to the rope with the aid of a belay device or body belay technique. The belayer has the ability to take in or let out slack to correspond with the movement of a climber. Under the heading of dynamic belays, High 5 uses two methods:

- the body (standing hip) belay, which uses the belayer's body and a gloved brake hand to gain friction

- mechanical device belays (Sticht plate, Trango Pyramid or Black Diamond ATC) which add friction to the system

An **AUSTRALIAN BELAY** is a system in which a group of individuals act as belayers. Protection for the climber is secured by clipping belayers into a tied loop (one option) at the ground end of the climbing rope.
As the climber moves up a tree or indoor wall, the belayers continuously back up maintaining tautness in the rope. This system is limited to obstacle free climbing set-ups. The belay on the Flying Squirrel is a modification of the Australian belay.

A **STATIC BELAY** is a fixed belay system in which a climber is clipped into an adjustable lanyard that is directly connected to the overhead belay set-up. The only example of a static belay on most High 5 challenge courses is the Zip Wire.

A **SELF-BELAY** system is one in which a climber manages her own safety usually through the use of an attached two-tethered safety lanyard, often referred to as lobster claws. The tethers of the lanyard are clipped alternatively into approved protection points during a climber's ascent.

Belaying is an important skill that must be taught in a logical progression beginning with the proper teaching of knots and use of equipment to ground school practice and finally actual climbing practice with backup systems.

Information in this chapter is not to be considered as a substitute for training, but as a means of review after training has occurred.

DYNAMIC BELAYS

The choice of belay technique reflects personal preference. A properly executed body belay is a low-tech method that provides a direct and safe connection between the climber and belayer. It is a good skill to know in the event of an emergency or if a mechanical belay device is not available. The majority of belayers prefer to use some type of mechanical belay device. (See Equipment for the High Challenge Course.) Belay devices enhance the friction in the belay system allowing some belayers to feel more confident, particularly for lighter persons belaying heavier participants. In High 5 workshops, we often introduce both methods so that workshop participants become familiar with both the body belay and at least one mechanical belay device system.

GENERAL GUIDELINES FOR THE BODY BELAY/ STANDING HIP BELAY

- The belay rope must run through at least one carabiner connected to the lower side or leg loop of the belayer's harness. This will help to keep the rope running underneath the belayer's buttocks giving added friction and control. If using just a single carabiner, the positioning of the single carabiner is always on the side (hip) opposite to the brake hand. Two carabiners may be used to further aid in keeping the rope beneath the buttocks. In this case, a carabiner would be positioned on each of the leg loops.

- To brake (lock down) the rope in the body belay, the brake hand moves the rope over the upper thigh and down toward the crotch.

- The belay position should be secure with one's weight equally distributed over the feet, knees comfortably flexed and feet spaced slightly wider than shoulders.

- Properly fitted gloves suitable for belaying should be worn. A glove on the brake hand is mandatory when using a body belay.

- The body belayer should avoid wearing pants or shorts made of synthetic material. The friction produced in belaying can quickly melt through these materials. Use an extra pair of larger shorts or leather belay chaps for added comfort.

- The appropriate back-up for a body belay is another body belay, with the back-up belayer standing at an angle in front of and facing the primary belayer (A position in the range of 9 to 11 o'clock is acceptable). This positioning results in bringing the belay rope across the belayer's body, causing the belayer to be caught in a loop of rope if the belay is dropped. The back-up belayer's gear must be set up in the same way as the primary belayer.

CAUGHT YOU THINKING #13:

True or False? The use of the body belay is a dated practice that should not be used in most programs.

Mechanical belay device

MECHANICAL BELAY DEVICES

There are many acceptable belay devices in use today. As previously mentioned, common examples are the slot-styled Sticht plate and the pyramid or tuber-styled Trango Pyramids, Black Diamond ATCs. A less common but highly effective belay device is the Just-Rite Descender traditionally used as the belay with trapeze-style events such as the Pamper Pole.

GENERAL GUIDELINES FOR MECHANICAL BELAY DEVICES

• To brake using a mechanical belay device, the brake hand pulls the rope down and to the side of the belay device in a smooth movement. This motion creates a crimping action on the rope, increasing friction and thus adding significant holding power.

• To back-up a belayer using a mechanical device, there are two options. One is for the back-up belayer to stand to the side and slightly behind the primary belayer. She will take in rope using both hands at the same rate as the primary belayer, taking care to leave enough slack in the rope, often referred to as a smile in the rope, so as to not interfere with the rope handling needs of the primary belayer. A second method has the back-up belayer taking in rope using a modified body belay. Positioning is the same for each. In both cases, eyes of the back-up belayer remain focused on the belayer.

• When a belay rope is properly run through a belay device, a reasonable amount of braking pressure applied by the belayer will normally stop a fall. However, if the rope is dropped, there will not be enough friction in the system to control a fall. It then becomes the job of the backup belayer to grip and hold the rope tightly with both hands, activating the belay device of the primary belayer.

• The use of gloves is optional when using a belay device. Gloves however can reduce wear and tear on hands particularly in lengthy belay sessions. Please note that poorly fitting gloves, as well as loose clothing and long hair, can get caught in belay devices causing them to jam.

• Some programs have used Figure Eight devices for belaying. Realize that many of these are lightweight and intended for rappelling use only. Only figure eight's designated suitable for belaying should be used. Figure eight's can cause kinks in the belay rope.

• When using commercially made harnesses, follow the manufacturer's instructions for the proper connection (clip in) point when using mechanical belay devices.

- Belay methods vary. High 5 currently teaches two techniques. One is the more traditional rope transfer method often known as Slip, Slap, Slide. The second is commonly referred to as the BUS method (Brake, Under, Slide). Both systems are acceptable. Proper training and practice are essential for appropriate development of these skills.

JUST-RITE DESCENDER

This unique belay system was originally designed by Karl Rohnke to allow a small person to have the confidence and competence to manage the belay on jumping elements like the Pamper Pole. The first Just-Rite Descender was an enormous log, 8' long and 14" wide sunk deeply into the ground. A series of 5 or 6 angled holes were hand drilled in the log through which the belay end of the rope was passed in a sequential top to bottom fashion. Friction from the rope running in this fashion through the openings aided the belayer in maintaining control of the rope. This first prototype worked exceptionally well and became the model for future Just-Rite descenders. Today, Just-Rite descenders are still sometimes used in conjunction with jumping events. Typically, lengths of telephone pole with somewhat fewer holes have replaced logs to increase longevity. A standing hip belay is the usual method used with this device. The belayer takes up her belay stance at the back of the pole, taking in slack as the climber ascends the pole. When the climber jumps, the belayer often takes a step or two back and to the side to reduce the accumulation of additional slack

Just-Rite Descenders vary in the amount of friction produced as aperture openings often differ: the wider the opening, the less the friction. Over time, as holes wear smooth, friction will likely also decrease. It is wise to first test an unfamiliar system to become comfortable with the feel of the belay.

A belay using a Just-Rite Descender

THE AUSTRALIAN BELAY

The Australian belay is a group belay method. Its use and acceptance in school programs has increased as it has been recognized as a practice that involves more participants in the belay process. Selling points for this system are its simplicity: in set-up, instruction and implementation. The Australian belay works through a system of counterbalanced weights. The weight of the climber is supported and off-set by the combined weights of several belayers. Each is tied in or attached to opposing ends of the climbing rope. It is important to note, however, that the Australian belay may not be a suitable belay method for all climbing elements. This technique requires considerable space on at least one side of the high element. (See belay system below). Indoor challenge courses and Pole courses in field settings are most compatible with this technique.

There are several acceptable ways to set up the Australian belay. High 5 trainers prefer the following methods:

SET-UP:

STEP I To begin, set up the climbing rope in a regular fashion. At the climber's end of the rope, tie a climbing knot with a back-up knot (bowline on a bight or double figure eight). At the belayer's end of the rope, tie a similar knot but this time make sure that the loops of the knot are large (at least a foot in length).

STEP 2 (Variation #1) At the belayer's end of the rope, splay open the two loops of the knot. Have the belayers each clip into one of the loops of the knot with a locking carabiner. For example, if there are four belayers, two will clip into one of the knot's loops while the remaining two will clip into the second loop. The loops need to be large enough to prevent overcrowding. If desired, additional students may be used to help pull on the belay rope. These students are not clipped directly into the system.

STEP 2 (Variation #2) At the belayer's end of the rope, again tie a climbing knot with large loops. Take pre-formed loops of either 9mm kernmantle rope or 1 inch tubular webbing and girth hitch them to the loops of the climbing knot. The pre-formed loops are approximately 2-3 feet in overall length. Each of the pre-formed loops must be properly tied with either a Double Fisherman's Knot (kernmantle rope) or a Water knot (webbing). Once attached to the climbing knot, the belayers each clip into one of the pre-formed loops with a locking carabiner.

OPERATIONAL GUIDELINES FOR THE AUSTRALIAN BELAY

In simplest terms, the Australian belay system works by having the belayers move slowly backwards as the climber advances upwards. Tension in the climbing rope is maintained at all times. The belayers always move in a direct line with the climber remaining parallel to her position on the climb. The lower is executed in reverse in the same way, a slow moving forward of the belayers to maintain a controlled descent.

- As with any belay system, a proper pre-climbing check must be completed.

- The number of belayers must outweigh the weight of the climber by a minimum ratio of 2:1. It is hard to come up with a firm number of belayers as weight ratios differ depending upon the age and size of the climber. In a school setting, often 4 - 6 students are used in the group belay.

- Footing for the belayers will vary depending upon the location of the climb. Floor surfaces in indoor settings may be very slippery. With less traction, it can become more difficult to counterbalance the weight of the climber particularly on the descent. Always err on the side of having more belayers to provide for smooth and safe belays.

- Communication with the belayer becomes more complex with a group belay. It is recommended that a belay team leader be established before each climb. This individual will be responsible for coordinating the movements of the belay team as well as communicating with the climber.

- Watch for overcrowding and bumping in the belay team. Each individual should have the space to move easily and safely forwards and backwards.

- The belay team should be focused on the climber at all times maintaining appropriate tension on the climbing rope. The belay team must be monitored and supervised by an instructor at all times.

- Although the Australian belay method requires no special hand techniques, participants must receive proper training and practice on the ground before use in actual climbing situations.

- The Australian belay may in some situations be used with traversing high elements. However, as this is considered a specialty skill, it is recommended that only mature and responsible belay teams who have received thorough training be allowed to belay in these circumstances.

A TEAM APPROACH FOR THE BELAY

A belay team approach for managing belay responsibilities promotes the concept of working together. High elements have been often been earmarked as individual challenges which is often contrary to the goals and objectives of challenge course programming. Dividing up the responsibilities in the belay strengthens the sense of community in the program and at the same time actively involves more participants. Possible roles in a belay team are:

Climber:	**Climbs the element**
Primary belayer:	**Is responsible for managing the belay**
Back-up belayer:	**Works with the belayer. Assumes belay responsibilities if belay fails for any reason**
Anchor:	**Holds harness or shoulders to stabilize belayer**
Tender:	**Manages excess rope; keeps it out of the way of the belayers**
Ladder spotter:	**Will hold the ladder as the climber ascends**

BEST BELAY PRACTICES

CLIPPING INTO THE BELAY

On challenge courses, standard locking carabiners have been typically used to connect the climbing rope to the climber's harness. This method is quick, easy to teach and easy to inspect. Most facilitators advocate orienting the carabiner so that the screw gate on the carabiner is in a downward – rotating position to take advantage of gravity's pull in maintaining a closed gate. This preference is derived from the "screw down so you won't screw up" challenge course mantra that refers to the rapid link positioning for belay set-ups. In the harness clip-in application, although it may make sense to follow along with established protocols for gate closures, what is most important here is that the gate be closed and checked.

Where to clip often becomes trickier: through the belay loop or not; use one or two carabiners; yes or no to clipping into the back of the harness? Each harness manufacturer has its own requirements as to how the harness may be used. It is essential that the manufacturer's instructions be learned and followed.

CAUGHT YOU THINKING #14:

I've heard that two carabiners should be used to clip climbers into the belay rope. Our program uses one. Which method is correct?

KNOTS FOR THE CLIP-IN

Typically, most challenge course sites have relied on one of the following three knots at the climber's end of the belay rope: the bowline on a bight , the double figure eight and the retraced figure eight. A double overhand back up knot placed within two inches or less of the primary knot is always used in challenge course programming.

BOWLINE ON A BIGHT One variation of the multi-purpose bowline knot is the bowline on a bight . This knot is strong, has a redundant coil, and is easy to untie after having been weighted. One down side to this knot is that a mistake slip version can be easily tied. The mistake knot is very similar to the correct knot and can require a trained critical eye to see the difference. The bowline on a bight needs to be well set and dressed, particularly in new rope as it has a tendency to loosen.

DOUBLE FIGURE EIGHT The double figure eight which is sometimes referred to as the super eight has gained acceptance in recent years. It is generally easier to tie than the bowline on a bight and still offers high knot strength and loop redundancy. It can be a bit more difficult to untie than the Bowline after being weighted.

RETRACED FIGURE EIGHT Some courses use a retraced figure eight to connect the climbing rope to the harness. Traditionally, this has been the preferred tie-in method for rock climbers as it eliminates a carabiner from the system and provides a secure connection that will remain tied even with rubbing against a rock surface. For this reason, some sites prefer to use it on certain high elements like the Dangle Duo or Vertical Playpen where body contact with the element's structure is likely.

KNOT WEB SITES

- http://www.animatedknots.com
- http://www.42brghtn.mistral.co.uk/knots/42ktmenu.html
- http://www.folsoms.net/knots/

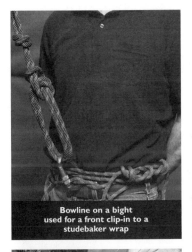

Bowline on a bight used for a front clip-in to a studebaker wrap

Double figure eight used for a front clip-in to a seat harness

Retraced figure eight knot used for a front clip-in to a seat harness

BELAY GUIDELINES
These guidelines apply for both the standing hip belay and the belay with a mechanical device.

- The braking hand should ALWAYS be closed around the rope.

- Proper tension in the belay line should be kept at all times. There is a balance between having excess slack or constant tension. Realize that the belay rope is there to protect the climber from harm and not to provide assistance to the climber unless the climber requests it.

- If a belayer cannot take in or let out rope to accommodate a climber's pace, the belayer should communicate to the climber to slow down.

- A belayer should be aware of the dynamic stretch of the climbing rope. A fall that occurs near the start of a climb (10 to 15 feet up) could result in ground contact if sufficient tension is not maintained in the belay.

- A belayer should move laterally with any participant who is traversing an element, keeping parallel to that person. Traverse with the participant, brake hand engaged, being alert to catch a fall at any time.

- At the start of a climb, a belayer should check to make sure that the belay set-ups are correctly positioned as directly over the climber as possible. In traversing elements, this may be difficult to do as the slight drape in the cable may prevent the belay equipment from sliding close to the access tree. A belayer should be alert to preventing a pendulum swing in the event of a climber's fall.

- The belayer should stand at a reasonable distance from the element (approx. 10-12 feet) Standing too far from the element may cause the belayer to be pulled forward in the event of a fall and risk possibly losing control of the rope.

- The belayer's attention should be focused on the climber at all times.

- Proper climbing signals or some other agreed upon verbal exchange should be used to maintain good, clear communication with the climber.

- An anchor (human or fixed) should be used if there is a significant weight differential between the climber and the belayer.

- Only competent and well-trained belayers should belay.

- Make sure the belay rope is properly positioned on the element and that the participant is clipped in on the proper side for a trouble free ascent. A climber should follow the path of the ascending rope. Belayers should watch for snags on staples, tree nubbins etc.

- Climbers should be lowered in a safe and controlled manner.

- A belayer must do a thorough check of the climber's equipment prior to the climb. This should include an examination for proper fitting of the helmet and harness, a locked carabiner and a properly tied climbing knot.

- Encourage climbers appropriately. Give climbers time to set reasonable goals. Honor their decisions. Ask climbers to indicate the type of support they want or don't want from the group such as verbal encouragement, silence, etc.

- Proper climbing signals or some other agreed upon verbal exchange should be used to maintain good, clear communication with the climber. The most commonly used climber/belayer exchange is as follows:

Climber:	**On belay? (Climber is clipped in and is ready to begin.)**
Belayer:	**Belay on. (Belayer has set up the belay and is ready to belay)**
Climber:	**Climbing? (Climber is asking for permission to start climbing)**
Belayer:	**Climb on. (Belayer grants permissions to climb)**

Other useful commands include "Tension" (please take up any slack in the rope), "Slack" (ease off slightly on the belay) and "Falling" (a heads-up to the belayer that the climber is about to fall). Also, at the conclusion of a climb, the commands, "Off belay" and "Belay off" are often used to indicate the end of the contract between climber and belayer. As it is often obvious on a challenge course when a belay is no longer needed (the climber is usually standing in front of you on the ground), this final exchange is a polite and respectful way to acknowledge the support given and is often accompanied by a "Thank you!"

OTHER HELPFUL INFORMATION ABOUT BELAY SYSTEMS

- Remember that there is a lot of give in a dynamic belay system, particularly in courses installed in trees. Belayers must be prepared for falls from a height of less than ten feet. A snug belay, proper belayer positioning, and the use of spotters can be prudent strategies for protecting starting climbers.

- A belay rope that is held very tight does not necessarily make the climber more secure. In fact, it may hinder the climber by throwing them off balance and inhibiting forward movement on traversing elements. Allow the participant a choice in determining the amount of slack in their belay rope, within safe perimeters.

- The best strategy for catching a fall may not be to lock down tight on the belay device. In certain cases the abrupt stopping of a fall will result in a pendulum swing. This happens when there is a very dynamic belay system. Best practice in this instance is to keep some pressure on the belay rope, letting the participant descend to below the element. At that point, a total brake can be applied or a continuation of a smooth belayed descent.

- Lowering methods from different elements may vary. The main purpose is to have participants descend in such a manner that they clear the obstacle without injury. A slow, controlled and smooth descent is critical.

- Participants may want to grab their belay rope for added security. It's okay, and often a good secure feeling for the climber to grab the rope attached directly in front of her. In a descent, holding onto the descending portion of the rope is fine. Grabbing the ascending portion of the rope may result in painful rope burn.

- Backup belayers are used to add greater security to the belay systems, most particularly with novice or student belayers. However, if backup belayers are not alert and/or properly trained, they may overreact and cause the brake hand of the primary belayer to be pulled away from her side. Backup belayers must remember that they act only if the primary belayer loses control of the belay rope

- Terrain can impact the safety of the belay. If an element is built on a slope, a belayer should try to stand on the downhill side of the element. If a fall occurs, the belayer is then pulled into the hill and a firm stance can be maintained. To the contrary, if a belayer stood on the uphill side of the element, a fall might cause the belayer to be pulled forward off the ground. This would result in a pendulum swing from the side of the hill toward the element. Such action might cause the belayer surprise and potentially a loss of control of the belay system.

- Also, if the terrain in a traversing element slopes up and down, be prepared to adjust the belay rope accordingly. Rope will need to be let out walking downhill and taken in on the uphill.

- Anchors may add more security to the system especially when belaying larger persons. Acceptable practices include having a group member hold onto a belayer's Studebaker Wrap or harness or to have a group member provide downward hand pressure on the belayer's shoulders. When the belayer is following the movement of a participant on a traversing element, the support crew needs to move with the belayer and not hinder or interfere with the belayer's hands or the free end of the belay rope. Securing or anchoring the belayer to a fixed point should not be attempted on any traversing belay because of the resulting pendulum fall that will result.

BELAY TRANSFERS

A belay transfer occurs when a climber switches from one belay system to another. Belay transfers from one element to another on dynamic courses are uncommon as most elements are run as separate challenges. However there are two common locations on a dynamic course where a transfer at height is possible. One is on the Zip Wire, transferring a climber from a dynamic belay to a static belay (the zip lanyard) and the second is at the top of a Climbing Tower where participants may choose to remain after a climb. In this case, the climber would move from a dynamic belay to a static lanyard or tether. For transfers at height, it is highly recommended that an instructor be present to monitor and check the new connections.

For the High 5 course, an instructor is required to be present on both the Zip Wire and Climbing Tower platforms to manage transfers.

GUIDELINES FOR USING PARTICIPANT BELAYERS

Participant belayers are program participants who either have not received extensive formal belay training or who are novice belayers in a training program. In both examples, it is assumed that participant belayers do not have the same qualified competence and training as an instructor. Therefore, the following protocols are strongly recommended.

- Participants should receive a thorough explanation of proper belaying procedures (hand movements, commands, use of equipment). Participants should practice these procedures on the ground before height is introduced.

- Training for participant belayers should be equivalent in length to that which a person would receive during a professional skills training workshop.

- A ground team with back-up belayers and anchors must be used.

- All participant belayers must be closely supervised by a qualified facilitator.

OPERATING PROCEDURES FOR HIGH CHALLENGE COURSE ELEMENTS AND INITIATIVES

The following section on High Challenge Course Elements details the standard operating procedures for many of the high elements built by High 5 Adventure Learning Center. It is important to recognize that individual challenge courses vary and that basic operational practices may require modification to meet the unique features of each course. Elements in this section are listed alphabetically.

BURMA BRIDGE

CATWALK

CENTIPEDE

CLIMBING TOWER

DANGLE DUO

FLYING SQUIRREL

HIGH Y

HOLY COW SWING

INCLINED LOG

JEEBIE LUNGE

KISSING TREE

MULTIVINE TRAVERSE

PAMPER POLE

PAMPER PLANK

PIRATE'S CROSSING

ROLL-OUT RAPPEL

SPACE LOOPS

STEMMING CLIMB

TWO LINE BRIDGE

TWO SHIPS CROSSING

VERTICAL PLAYPEN

ZIP WIRE

USER GUIDE:

Elements in this section are listed alphabetically. The information about each element is subdivided into the following categories and includes the elements listed below:

ELEMENT NAME
Brief description of the element.

SET UP
The belay set-ups for each element are briefly described.

TASK
A suggested goal is listed for each element.

FACILITATOR'S ROLE
This section addresses the major responsibilities for a belayer before a climb on any element. The same checklist will appear with each high element listed in the High Challenge Course section. This is to emphasize the importance of a thorough and complete check of a climber's equipment prior to each and every climb.

ELEMENT SPECIFIC GUIDELINES
Element specific instructions are listed in this section. These may include spotting guidelines, tips on belayer positioning, or things to watch carefully during the belay. Every element is constructed slightly differently and may often require procedural modifications. For example, no two Pamper Poles are exactly alike and are therefore belayed slightly differently. It is important to become familiar with each element on a course and to adapt the operating guidelines to their unique qualities.

VARIATIONS
Alternative ways of using or presenting an element.

BURMA BRIDGE

This element features a V-shaped bridge formed by a foot cable and 2 multi-line hand rails.

SET UP

Set up from the top down on the belay cable: stainless steel pulley; 12mm rapid link; stainless steel SR device.

TASK

To walk across the foot cable using the two hand lines for support.

FACILITATOR'S ROLE

- Complete the pre-climbing check.

- Visually check to see that belay set-ups are properly oriented.

- Check the knot in the end of the belay rope.

- Visually check that a locking carabiner has been properly clipped into the harness or around all the strands of the Studebaker Wrap. It should be locked and squeeze checked.

- Before climbing, check that the harness or Studebaker Wrap is belted or tied correctly according to manufacturer's recommendations.

- Make sure that the participant is wearing a correctly sized helmet and that it is put on properly.

- Follow all belay guidelines described under Best Belay Practices on page 108.

ELEMENT SPECIFIC GUIDELINES

- Make sure that the climbing rope is set up properly so that the climber has a direct path to the cable and does not have to climb over one of the Burma Bridge hand lines.

- When lowering climbers from the Burma Bridge, have them position themselves for the descent so that the climbing rope will be properly situated for the next climber. The climber should descend underneath the hand line.

CATWALK

A horizontally positioned pole or log suspended between two trees. The belay cable is positioned above the log, parallel to the ground and at a height of nine to ten feet above the log.

SET UP
Set up from the top down on the belay cable: stainless steel pulley; 12 mm rapid link; stainless steel SR device.

TASK
The challenge is to walk across the log. The belay rope may be used for balance if desired.

FACILITATOR'S ROLE
- Complete the pre-climbing check.

- Visually check to see that belay set-ups are properly oriented.

- Check the knot in the end of the belay rope.

- Visually check that a locking carabiner has been properly clipped into the harness or around all the strands of the Studebaker Wrap. It should be locked and squeeze checked.

- Before climbing, check that the harness or Studebaker Wrap is belted or tied correctly according to manufacturer's recommendations.

- Make sure that the participant is wearing a correctly sized helmet and that it is put on properly.

- Follow all belay guidelines described under Best Belay Practices in this manual.

ELEMENT SPECIFIC GUIDELINES
- Set up the element in such a way that the belayer can follow the traversing participant freely.

- Lower a climber smoothly off the Cat Walk being careful to prevent the climber from banging against the beam.

CENTIPEDE

The Centipede is a vertically hanging high element composed of individual 4 x 4 x 8 foot stapled lengths of wood linked together to create a dynamic climbing challenge.

SET UP
Set up from the top down on the belay cable: 12 mm rapid link; stainless steel SR device.

TASK
The challenge is to climb the swaying element using the randomly placed staples. The challenge may be made easier by having a spotter hold the base of the apparatus.

FACILITATOR'S ROLE
- Complete the pre-climbing check.

- Visually check to see that belay set-ups are properly oriented.

- Check the knot in the end of the belay rope.

- Visually check that a locking carabiner has been properly clipped into the harness or around all the strands of the Studebaker Wrap. It should be locked and squeeze checked.

- Before climbing, check that the harness or Studebaker Wrap is belted or tied correctly according to manufacturer's recommendations.

- Make sure that the participant is wearing a correctly sized helmet and that it is put on properly.

- Follow all belay guidelines described under Best Belay Practices on page 108.

ELEMENT SPECIFIC GUIDELINES
- The belayer must monitor the climber closely to make sure she follows the path of the belay rope to avoid wraps and twists around the Centipede.

- To add stability for the climber, a spotter may be used to hold the base of the Centipede. It is recommended that the spotter wear a helmet.

- When lowering a climber, have a participant pull the Centipede to the side to allow for a clear descent.

VARIATIONS
Two centipedes hung side by side create an element called Synchronicity. Two participants each on one of the Centipedes climb in tandem linked by a Velcro strap attached to the wrist. The goal is to both climb and be lowered without ever breaking the tenuous connection.

CLIMBING TOWER

A climbing tower is a challenge course structure usually built with telephone pole supports that can rise as high as 40 feet in the air. Tower designs vary offering multiple options. Climbing surfaces may feature overhangs and chimneys or rappelling walls. Ropes course elements can be either hung from the tower structure itself or set off at angles towards adjacent poles. Most 3 or 4 pole towers also feature a decked platform at the top of the structure, a place from which instructors can oversee and manage participant safety. The safety practices for a tower vary depending upon the design and complexity of the structure. Basic tower management practices will be described here. Specific training is recommended for each specific site due to the variation in design. At the top of the tower, backed up belay cables connect each of the telephone poles. Belay and rappel set-ups are hung from these cables.

TOWER: CLIMBING WALL

SET UP
Set up from the top down on the belay cable: 12mm rapid link; stainless steel SR device. (For two climbing routes, install 2 sets separated by a PVC pipe.)

TASK
To climb the vertical face using the attached climbing holds. The holds may be arranged in specific route patterns.

FACILITATOR'S ROLE
• Complete the pre-climbing check.

• Visually check to see that belay set-ups are properly oriented.

• Check the knot in the end of the belay rope.

• Visually check that a locking carabiner has been properly clipped into the harness or around all the strands of the Studebaker Wrap. It should be locked and squeeze checked.

• Before climbing, check that the harness or Studebaker Wrap is belted or tied correctly according to manufacturer's recommendations.

- Make sure that the participant is wearing a correctly sized helmet and that it is put on properly.

- Follow all belay guidelines described under Best Belay Practices on page 108.

ELEMENT SPECIFIC GUIDELINES

Climbers should be instructed to not stray too far to the right or left of the belay set-up particularly as they near the top of the climbing wall. A fall from such a position would result in a pendulum swing for the climber.

TOWER: RAPPEL

Often one face of the tower is designed for rappelling. This upper third of the rappel face is most often covered with decking. The lower section is open.

TASK

Rappelling is the skill of sliding down a rope using friction to control the rate of descent. On High 5 courses, the person on rappel is also on a belay rope that serves as a back-up system. An instructor positioned on top of the platform helps the participant into the correct rappel position. A second instructor manages the belay either from the ground or the top of the tower.

SET-UP

ROPES:

- BELAY ROPE: In all High 5 programs, participants are belayed during a rappel. The belay serves as a back-up system in case the participant on rappel loses control of the rappel or experiences a jamming of the rappel system. The belay system is set up on the belay cable with a rapid link and standard SR device.

- **RAPPEL:** Generally, static rope is used for rappel rope. A static rope features high tensile strength, low stretch, and low spinning tendencies which are key factors for the rappel. The rappel rope may be set up as a single strand or doubled to form two strands. The doubled rope setup significantly increases the friction potential in the system. A single strand is usually sufficient on a short rappel that has a backup belay. This rappel rope can be clipped onto the belay cable with a rapid link or steel carabiner using a double figure 8 knot. (For alternative set-up, see Anchors below)

RAPPEL HARDWARE:

The figure eight is probably the most popular rappelling device although other belay devices can also be used in a rappel. Both work by creating friction between the rope and the belay device.

ANCHORS:

There will be two separate and independent systems for the belay and the rappel. It is recommended that the rappel be set up so that the rappel rope could be easily loosened if necessary to relieve any jams in the system. Jams could be caused by hair or clothing that gets caught in the rappel hardware. If a jam were to occur in the rappel line, tension first is taken up on the belay line. Next, the rappel line is loosened and a slight amount of slack is eased into the rappel rope. When enough slack develops, the person on rappel will be held in position by the belay rope. At this point, the rappeller can then remove the jam. Setups for this type of rappel lowering system vary. Proper training and instruction in a method best suited to each individual tower set-up is recommended.

RAPPEL TECHNIQUES

- Make sure the person who is going to rappel fully understands the mechanics of the rappel device and knows how to properly position her hand to control the rate of descent.

- Use proper communication signals. Make sure that the rappeller first goes on belay before attempting to rappel.

- Encourage the participant to move slowly into the rappel, making sure that there is adequate tension on the rappel rope and that the brake hand is applying sufficient friction.

- Instruct the rappeller to back over the lip of the platform with feet that are approximately shoulder width apart for balance. Encourage the participant to lean back in an L-shaped position keeping feet in positive contact with The Wall. Forward lean will cause the feet to slide out from under the body potentially causing the rappeller to bump into The Wall.

- Progress should be smooth and slow. If part of the rappel is a free rappel whereby the rappeller is hanging in space, instruct the participant to maintain a comfortable sitting position.

- Gloves are recommended for the rappel participant. Gloves protect the hands both from simple abrasion as the rope passes through them and from heat built up from friction in the rappel device.

FACILITATOR'S ROLE

Before this event, cover the basic elements of the rappel on the ground. Participants should practice this skill before attempting it at height.

- Complete the pre-climbing check.

- Visually check to see that belay set-ups are properly oriented.

- Check the knot in the end of the belay rope.

- Visually check that a locking carabiner has been properly clipped into the harness or around all the strands of the Studebaker Wrap. It should be locked and squeeze checked.

- Before climbing, check that the harness or Studebaker Wrap is belted or tied correctly according to manufacturer's recommendations.

- Make sure that the participant is wearing a correctly sized helmet and that it is put on properly.

- Follow all belay guidelines described under Best Belay Practices in this manual.

ELEMENT SPECIFIC GUIDELINES

- All loose clothing and long hair (anything that could get caught in the rappel device) should be secured before attempting the rappel.

- Monitor the belay rope on the participant's ascent to make sure the climber follows the path of the rope.

- During the rappel, the back-up belayer should keep a loose belay so that the participant can descend at her own rate. Too much tension in the belay will make it difficult for the rappeller to maintain a correct position and rate of descent. Rappels should be smooth and not overly fast.

DANGLE DUO

A vertically hung, oversized ladder suspended from an overhead cable or clipped directly into support trees or poles. The rungs are usually 4 x 4 x 8 pressure treated boards. A separate belay cable is suspended seven feet above the uppermost log.

SET UP

Set up from the top down on the belay cable: 12 mm rapid link, stainless steel SR device (Install 2 sets separated by a PVC pipe). A Dangle Trio or Quad would require three and four belay set-ups accordingly.

TASK

The Dangle Duo is generally used as a partner activity in which participants climb the ladder using only the support of the logs and/or each other. Use of the side support cables is discouraged.

FACILITATOR'S ROLE

• Complete the pre-climbing check.

• Visually check to see that belay set-ups are properly oriented.

• Check the knot in the end of the belay rope.

• Visually check that a locking carabiner has been properly clipped into the harness or around all the strands of the Studebaker Wrap. It should be locked and squeeze checked.

• Before climbing, check that the harness or Studebaker Wrap is belted or tied correctly according to manufacturer's recommendations.

• Make sure that the participant is wearing a correctly sized helmet and that it is put on properly.

• Follow all belay guidelines described under Best Belay Practices on page 108.

ELEMENT SPECIFIC GUIDELINES

- Have spotters spot each participant when mounting the first rung (especially if the rung is close to the ground). Rope stretch at this point may prevent a belayer from arresting a ground fall.

- Do not allow participants to climb in such a way that their belay rope gets wrapped around a rung.

- To lower participants, have someone pull the Dangle Duo out of the way (out of plumb) to create a clear path to the ground. This can also be done by looping a rope over the bottom rung and pulling it away from the descending climbers. If there are two climbers, it is best to lower them one at a time.

FLYING SQUIRREL

The Flying Squirrel is an element that gives a participant an opportunity to be lifted in the air on a static line by members of the group. The lift can be either a straight vertical raise or a swinging motion if the participant takes a short run as she is being pulled into the air.

SET UP

Two cables are strung between two trees or utility poles. On the bottom cable, a rapid link with an attached cable pulley is fixed at a midpoint on the cable. The upper backed up belay cable has a rapid link with a short attached swaged-looped cable. This cable length is connected to the lower rapid link providing back-up for the Flying Squirrel system.

TASK

TO BE LIFTED OFF THE GROUND (NO SWING):

- A volunteer squirrel (climber) clips a locking carabiner into the front of her harness or Studebaker Wrap.

- On a signal from the instructor, the hauling group begins to slowly back up pulling the participant off the ground.

- At a halfway point, the participant is allowed a choice as to whether to continue or to descend from that point.

TO BE A REAL FLYING SQUIRREL:

- Change the clip-in point to the back of a combination chest harness and seat harness or Studebaker Wrap. A full-body harness with a back clip could also be used. If a commercial harness is used, it must be the Headwall Universal harness or one that has been specifically manufactured for use with back clips.

- Have the rest of the group (minimum eight people) hold the other end of the rope. A minimum of two members of the group are clipped into the end of the rope with either a bowline on a bight or a double figure eight knot (sometimes the loops are split). To provide additional grip on the belay end of the rope, an option is to tie butterfly knots at intervals along the belay rope. If this is done, it is important to avoid a situation where pullers may trip over one another. This can be avoided by simply limiting the number of butterfly knots.

An alternative set-up that is useful in a smaller than average gymnasium with limited space for a pulling team is to use an Australian belay set-up with tethers. Four to six participants are clipped into the tethers radiating from the belay knot. They will serve as anchors for the system. The remaining participants will hold onto the belay rope for additional pull and support. The Australian belay team should use caution when moving backward to avoid crowding each other.

To begin the launch process, have the participant back up a few steps towards the pulling group from her position directly underneath the belay set-up. After proper commands, have the participant then run in the opposite direction away from the hauling group. It is important for the participant to run straight and not at an angle. This will avoid a spiraling swinging motion. At the same time the pulling group also moves out smartly away from the flyer, pulling the participant into the air. Once the participant is safely off the ground, the group should slow its forward momentum. Excessive and fast pulling action will result in unsafe swinging of the participant. Upward pulling of the participant must stop at such a point that there is no risk of the participant coming in contact with the belay cable.

FACILITATOR'S ROLE

- Complete the pre-climbing check.

- Visually check to see that belay set-ups are properly oriented.

- Check the knot in the end of the belay rope.

- Visually check that a locking carabiner has been properly clipped into the harness or around all the strands of the Studebaker Wrap. It should be locked and squeeze checked.

- Before climbing, check that the harness or Studebaker Wrap is belted or tied correctly according to manufacturer's recommendations.

- Make sure that the participant is wearing a correctly sized helmet and that it is put on properly.

- Follow all belay guidelines described under Best Belay Practices in this manual.

ELEMENT SPECIFIC GUIDELINES

- Use climbing commands between the "squirrel" and the belay team.

- Pay attention to the height of the flyer. Her maximum height should be far enough below the belay cable to prevent any possibility of hitting the cable or flipping over the cable. A tennis ball could be affixed to the flying squirrel rope approximately 4-5' from the participant. This marker on the rope could then serve as a visual reminder to the group to stop pulling. This also would reduce the possibility of a person from getting pulled too high. It is best to designate one member of the belay team (or the instructor) to call "STOP" to the pulling group when the squirrel has reached maximum height.

- A long pendulum glide results when the flyer is raised less than halfway to the pulley.

- As the participant descends, have a greeter be there to offer a supporting hand. This helps to steady the participant and to slow the swinging motion.

HIGH Y

A Wild Woosey built high in the trees. The configuration for this element mirrors the low element in that two diverging foot cables fan out from a common starting point forming a V. Overhead cables that are slightly inset from the foot cables provide protection points for the climbers.

SET UP

Set up from the top down on each of the belay cables: stainless steel cable pulley, 12 mm rapid link stainless steel SR device.

TASK

This is a challenge for two people to traverse as far out on the angled cables as possible using only each other in the process.

FACILITATOR'S ROLE

- Complete the pre-climbing check.

- Visually check to see that belay set-ups are properly oriented.

- Check the knot in the end of the belay rope.

- Visually check that a locking carabiner has been properly clipped into the harness or around all the strands of the Studebaker Wrap. It should be locked and squeeze checked.

- Before climbing, check that the harness or Studebaker Wrap is belted or tied correctly according to manufacturer's recommendations.

- Make sure that the participant is wearing a correctly sized helmet and that it is put on properly.

- Follow all belay guidelines described under Best Belay Practices in this manual.

ELEMENT SPECIFIC GUIDELINES

- A back clip on this event is preferred as it keeps the belay rope out of the faces of the traversing pair. For this, a chest harness is strongly recommended in conjunction with a seat harness. The chest harness should be correctly fitted to the participant and connected to the seat harness and rope properly.

- The two climbers will access the High Y from the inside of the cables on staples that lead up the tree or pole through the space between the foot cables. Make sure the belay ropes are aligned properly for this approach.

- Set up the element in such a way that the belayers can follow the traversing participants freely.

- As the belay cables are slightly inset from the foot cables, belayers need to stand far enough back from the element to eliminate any potential rubbing of the belay rope on the foot cable.

HOLY COW SWING

An exhilarating swing through the air. Cables suspended from three over-head placements terminate in a single point and are connected by a large metal ring. A Multi-line lanyard hung from this ring provides a clip-in point for a participant, who can then be pulled to height via a releasable haul system that is activated by group members. Once the participant has pulled the release, a long sweeping swing ensues.

SET UP

The set-up can vary from site to site. Following are general directions for the operation of this event. Always get specific site training instructions prior to using this activity.

TO SET UP THE HAUL SYSTEM:

- Using a lazy line, hoist up the Holy Cow haul rope (KM3 static rope).

- At one end of the haul rope, tie a backed up double figure 8 or bowline on a bight . This end will be the clip in point for the swinger.

- Tie a butterfly knot in the haul system rope approximately 4-5 feet from the clip-in point for the participant.

- Attach a 3/8" multi-line retrieval rope to the butterfly knot with a small clip.

- Attach a pulley with a rapid link or carabiner to the NEB at the base of the haul tree. (NEB at the base of a tree if outdoors or wall anchor if inside.)

- Reeve the other end of the haul rope through the pulley. Set up the pull so that participants can move in a unobstructed path at an angle to the swinger (and clear from the swinger.)

TO SET UP THE SWING LANYARD:

Use a locking carabiner to attach the top end of the Holy Cow swing lanyard to the large metal ring that links the three overhead cables. The participant will clip into the bottom part of the lanyard also with a locking carabiner.

TASK

To pull a participant up to her desired height and have that participant pull a release system activating the swing. If you listen closely, you may hear a "Holy Cow."

FACILITATOR'S ROLE

- Complete the pre-climbing check.

- Visually check to see that belay set-ups are properly oriented.

- Check the knot in the end of the belay rope.

- Visually check that a locking carabiner has been properly clipped into the har-ness or around all the strands of the Studebaker Wrap. It should be locked and squeeze checked.

- Before climbing, check that the harness is belted according to manufacturer's recommendations.

- Make sure that the participant is wearing a correctly sized helmet and that it is put on properly.

- Follow all belay guidelines described under Best Belay Practices on page 108.

ELEMENT SPECIFIC GUIDELINES

- No Studebakers wraps are to be used on the Holy Cow Swing. Rope abrasion can result from the dynamics of the swinging motion.

- Front clip-ins are preferred for the swing.

- To operate the swing, follow these procedures:

  – Place a step ladder beneath the clip in point. Have a participant climb up the step ladder. Make sure it is spotted by other participants.

  – Have the participant clip their harness into the fixed triangular rapid link at the end of the Holy Cow lanyard with a locking carabiner. Lock it shut.

  – Open the snap shackle (also attached to fixed rapid link) and place the double figure 8 (or bowline on a bight) knot of the haul line into opening. Snap shut. Make sure ropes are not crossed and will run smoothly.

  – Place a significant number of pullers on haul line. Prepare them for the pull and the eventual release. (They will topple over if they don't have a good stance at the time of release.)

  – Have one participant manage the retrieval line. That person should be standing off to the opposite side of the pullers holding the rope loosely or at the end.

  – MAKE SURE THAT THERE ARE NO ROPES THAT COULD BE TANGLED WITH THE SWINGER WHEN SHE RELEASES THE SYSTEM.

  – Have the participant step off of the ladder, hanging free.

  – Take away the step ladder.

  – Activate the pullers. Have them pull the participant up to her desired height.

  – Have the participant tug on the small white line attached to the snap shackle, pulling towards her to open the snap shackle. It is recommended that the swinger turn her head at this moment to ensure that there is no facial contact with the snap shackle.

  – Allow the participant to swing freely. When the swinger's momentum is slowing, gently tap the swinger's legs to reduce the speed. Having the swinger cross her ankles helps to provide a solid point of contact for the spotters and prevents excessive pulling on the legs. Bring the participant to a stop. Move in the step ladder and help the participant stand steadily on the ladder before unclipping.

  – Pull down on retrieval rope to prepare for connecting to the next swinger.

INCLINED LOG

A large diameter log rises at a low angle to a supported and secure anchor in an adjacent tree or pole. A horizontal belay cable is strung overhead slightly offset from the line of the log so that any falls or lowering off the log will remain clear of the element.

SET UP

Set up from the top down on the belay cable: stainless steel belay pulley, 12mm rapid link, stainless steel SR device.

TASK

A belayed participant attempts to walk the length of the log from bottom to top, trying all the while to remain in an upright walking position.

FACILITATOR'S ROLE

• Complete the pre-climbing check.

• Visually check to see that belay set-ups are properly oriented.

• Check the knot in the end of the belay rope.

• Visually check that a locking carabiner has been properly clipped into the harness or around all the strands of the Studebaker Wrap. It should be locked and squeeze checked.

• Before climbing, check that the harness or Studebaker Wrap is belted or tied correctly according to manufacturer's recommendations.

• Make sure that the participant is wearing a correctly sized helmet and that it is put on properly.

• Follow all belay guidelines described under Best Belay Practices in this manual.

ELEMENT SPECIFIC GUIDELINES

- Encourage the participant to ascend the inclined log in an upright posture rather than creeping along in an astride position. Allow only a front clip or tie-in.

- Know that if the belay rope is used for support by the climber, it may make it more difficult to maintain proper tension on the belay rope.

- Make sure that there are two to four spotters who spot the climber up the log until she has reached a six-foot level.

- If the climber reaches the top of the log, have her come down a few steps before being belayed down.

JEEBIE LUNGE

This challenge is represented by a taut, horizontal foot cable with an overhead parallel belay cable. Approximately, three-quarters of the way across the belay cable from the start, an eight-foot length of 3/4" Multi-line is hung. Additionally, a section of angled 5/8" Multi-line extends from the support tree at the start to a location on the foot cable approximately four feet short of the hanging 3/4" Multi-line.

SET UP

Set up from the top down on the belay cable: stainless steel belay pulley, 12mm rapid link, stainless steel SR device.

TASK

The belayed participant attempts to make her way out on the foot cable using the angled rope for support. Where the angled rope meets the cable, the climber then makes a lunge for the dangling rope. If a catch is made, the climber continues along the foot cable, using the grasped rope as a tension traverse, until the far support tree is achieved.

FACILITATOR'S ROLE

• Complete the pre-climbing check.

• Visually check to see that belay set-ups are properly oriented.

• Check the knot in the end of the belay rope.

• Visually check that a locking carabiner has been properly clipped into the harness or around all the strands of the Studebaker Wrap. It should be locked and squeeze checked.

• Before climbing, check that the harness or Studebaker Wrap is belted or tied correctly according to manufacturer's recommendations.

• Make sure that the participant is wearing a correctly sized helmet and that it is put on properly.

• Follow all belay guidelines described under Best Belay Practices in this manual.

ELEMENT SPECIFIC GUIDELINES

- Alert the belayer to the necessity of traversing with the climber. When the lunge is attempted, the belayer should be situated toward the start support tree to preclude a zipping of the belay pulley toward and into the far support tree.
- Belayers should pay attention to the climber's foot position prior to the lunge. Caution the climber not to have a foot tucked tightly in the acute angle formed by the cable and Multi-line rope.
- Participants should be cautioned not to grab the foot cable if they miss the rope when they lunge.

KISSING TREE

A kissing tree is one that naturally grows at a slightly off-vertical angle.

SET UP

Set up from the top down on the belay cable: stainless steel pulley, 12mm rapid link, stainless steel SR device.

TASK

The challenge of the kissing tree is to climb the amply stapled tree using one's hands as little as possible. A rope or cut tire segment slung around the tree may be employed as a climbing aid.

FACILITATOR'S ROLE

- Complete the pre-climbing check.

- Visually check to see that belay set-ups are properly oriented.

- Check the knot in the end of the belay rope.

- Visually check that a locking carabiner has been properly clipped into the harness or around all the strands of the Studebaker Wrap. It should be locked and squeeze checked.

- Before climbing, check that the harness or Studebaker Wrap is belted or tied correctly according to manufacturer's recommendations.

- Make sure that the participant is wearing a correctly sized helmet and that it is put on properly.

- Follow all belay guidelines described under Best Belay Practices in this manual.

MULTIVINE TRAVERSE

A foot cable with a series of Multi-line ropes suspended from an overhead cable. Each multi-line rope is purposefully positioned just beyond reach.

SET UP
Set up from the top down on the belay cable: stainless steel pulley, 12mm rapid link, stainless steel SR device. If this element is to be set up for two participants, a second separate belay cable is installed.

TASK
To walk across the foot cable using the various support rope vines for aid.

FACILITATOR'S ROLE
- Complete the pre-climbing check.

- Visually check to see that belay set-ups are properly oriented.

- Check the knot in the end of the belay rope.

- Visually check that a locking carabiner has been properly clipped into the harness or around all the strands of the Studebaker Wrap. It should be locked and squeeze checked.

- Before climbing, check that the harness or Studebaker Wrap is belted or tied correctly according to manufacturer's recommendations.

- Make sure that the participant is wearing a correctly sized helmet and that it is put on properly.

- Follow all belay guidelines described under Best Belay Practices on page 108.

ELEMENT SPECIFIC GUIDELINES
- Set up the element in such a way that the belayer can move easily with the traversing participant. Watch to make sure that the rope vines do not tangle with the belay rope.

- The belayer must be positioned and alert to the possibility of a pendulum fall.

PAMPER POLE

A leap to a suspended trapeze or target from a small perch on the top of a pole.

SET UP

From the top down on the belay cable: 12 mm rapid link, stainless steel SR device.

TASK

This activity involves climbing to the top of a pole, standing on top of a small platform and then, if desired, diving out to a trapeze suspended from a cable.

FACILITATOR'S ROLE

• Complete the pre-climbing check.

• Visually check to see that belay set-ups are properly oriented.

• Check the knot in the end of the belay rope.

• Visually check that a locking carabiner has been properly clipped into the harness or around all the strands of the Studebaker Wrap. It should be locked and squeeze checked.

• Before climbing, check that the harness or Studebaker Wrap is belted or tied correctly according to manufacturer's recommendations.

• Make sure that the participant is wearing a correctly sized helmet and that it is put on properly.

• Follow all belay guidelines described under Best Belay Practices in this manual.

ELEMENT SPECIFIC GUIDELINES

• A back clip on this event is preferred as it keeps the belay rope out of the way of the jumping climber. A chest harness is strongly recommended. This should be correctly fitted to the participant and connected to the seat harness and rope properly.

- The belay for the Pamper Pole can be set up in two ways. One option is to use a Just-Rite Descender, a log pole securely planted in the ground generally to the right of the element. The Just-Rite Descender serves as a belay device as it has several holes drilled through its width at various angles. The climbing rope is reeved through these holes starting from the top hole nearest the jump and then following a continuous in and out path until its final exit on the far side of the jump. The friction gained from the rope passing over the log surfaces provides the holding power for the belay. A best belay practice for the Just-Rite Descender is to use a body belay. The belayer takes a position directly behind the pole and draws in the slack as the climber ascends. On the jump, the belayer may choose to take a couple of steps back and to the side to reduce the slack in the rope. The lower is a smooth slow release of rope through the belay log. An alternative belay method is for the belayer to anchor herself directly to an anchor bolt placed in a tree facing the trapeze using either a short piece of webbing and a carabiner or a carabiner alone. One modification of this latter system is to attach the belay device directly to the anchor bolt. In this case, the anchor bolt must be backed up.

- Belayers should be prepared to take in slack quickly when the jumper leaps to diminish the amount of free fall after a missed jump.

- Climbers should be cautioned to spot themselves off the Pamper Pole after a jump, particularly if there is a big swing.

- If a climber catches the trapeze, she should be instructed to let go when the trapeze bar is swinging away from the Pamper Pole.

- Some Pamper Pole elements feature an In-line Trapeze bar adjustment whereby the trapeze can be moved via a pulley system to the desired jumping distance.

PAMPER PLANK

A leap to a suspended trapeze or target from a platform.

SET UP
From the top down on the belay cable: 12 mm rapid link, stainless steel SR device.

TASK
To climb a tree or a pole to a small platform. From there, if desired, to dive out to a trapeze suspended from a cable.

FACILITATOR'S ROLE
- Complete the pre-climbing check.

- Visually check to see that belay set-ups are properly oriented.

- Check the knot in the end of the belay rope.

- Visually check that a locking carabiner has been properly clipped into the harness or around all the strands of the Studebaker Wrap. It should be locked and squeeze checked.

- Before climbing, check that the harness or Studebaker Wrap is belted or tied correctly according to manufacturer's recommendations.

- Make sure that the participant is wearing a correctly sized helmet and that it is put on properly.

- Follow all belay guidelines described under Best Belay Practices in this manual.

ELEMENT SPECIFIC GUIDELINES

- A back clip on this event is preferred as it keeps the belay rope out of the way of the jumping climber. A chest harness is strongly recommended. This should be correctly fitted to the participant and connected to the seat harness and rope properly.

- The belay for the Pamper Plank can be set up in two ways. One option is to use a Just-Rite Descender, a log pole securely planted in the ground generally to the right of the element. The Just-Rite Descender serves as a belay device as it has several holes drilled through its width at various angles. The climbing rope is reeved through these holes starting from the top hole nearest the jump and then following a continuous in and out path until its final exit on the far side of the jump. The friction gained from the rope passing over the log surfaces provides the holding power for the belay. A best belay practice for the Just-Rite Descender is to use a body belay. The belayer takes a position directly behind the pole and draws in the slack as the climber ascends. On the jump, the belayer may choose to take a couple of steps back and to the side to reduce the slack in the rope. The lower is a smooth slow release of rope through the belay log. An alternative belay method is for the belayer to anchor herself directly to an anchor bolt placed in the tree facing the trapeze using either a short piece of webbing and a carabiner or a carabiner alone. One modification of this latter system is to attach the belay device directly to the anchor bolt. In this case, the anchor bolt must be backed up.

- Belayers should be prepared to take in slack quickly when the jumper leaps to diminish the amount of free fall after a missed jump.

- Climbers should be cautioned to spot themselves off the Pamper Plank after a jump, particularly if there is a big swing.

- If a climber catches the trapeze, she should be instructed to let go when the trapeze bar is swinging away from the Pamper Plank.

- Some Pamper Plank elements feature an In-line Trapeze bar adjustment whereby the trapeze can be moved via a pulley system to the desired jumping distance.

PIRATE'S CROSSING

Two Multi-line ropes create a large X in the center of this element. These intersecting lines each connect both to the foot cable and one of the support trees. The belay cable runs overhead parallel to the foot cable.

SETUP

Set up from the top down on the belay cable: stainless steel pulley, 12mm rapid link, stainless steel SR device.

TASK

To walk across the foot cable using the Multi-line ropes as aids to negotiate the difficult center section.

FACILITATOR'S ROLE

• Complete the pre-climbing check.

• Visually check to see that belay set-ups are properly oriented.

• Check the knot in the end of the belay rope.

• Visually check that a locking carabiner has been properly clipped into the harness or around all the strands of the Studebaker Wrap. It should be locked and squeeze checked.

• Before climbing, check that the harness or Studebaker Wrap is belted or tied correctly according to manufacturer's recommendations.

• Make sure that the participant is wearing a correctly sized helmet and that it is put on properly.

• Follow all belay guidelines described under Best Belay Practices in this manual.

ELEMENT SPECIFIC GUIDELINES

Falls tend to occur in the center of the climb at the X. Pay attention to the positioning of the climber's feet to make sure that they do not get stuck in the acute angle formed by the foot cable and the multi-line rope.

THE ROLL-OUT RAPPEL (ROR)

The Roll-out Rappel involves stepping off a platform placed high in the trees. A participant climbs on belay to a small perch in the tree. An instructor on the platform greets the climber and helps her clip into a rappel system (staying on belay throughout the process). Once set, the climber loads the rappel system (back-up belay system remains attached). As the rappel set-up includes a pulley, the participant gets an exhilarating ride to the middle of the cable prior to her descent on the rappel line.

SET UP

SET UP FROM TOP DOWN:
BELAY: A stainless steel pulley, a 12 mm rapid link, a Shear Reduction device

RAPPEL: A stainless steel pulley, a 12 mm rapid link. A single or double line rappel rope is clipped to this rapid link with an approved climbing clip-in knot. A single line is usually adequate for the ROR as the participant is always on belay. However, if more friction is desired in the rappel system, use a double rope set-up.

Two ropes are needed for the Roll-out Rappel, a belay rope and a rope for rappelling. The rappel rope is usually KM3, a static rope. In setting up this element, the belay rope system is outside the rappel rope system, further from the platform.

TASK
To climb to the small platform and with an instructor's help, set-up the rolling rappel rope. When ready, the climber exits the platform, rides out on the pulley and then begins the rappel. The belay serves as a back-up system.

FACILITATOR'S ROLE
• Before this event, cover the basic elements of the rappel on the ground. Participants should practice this skill before attempting it at height.

• All loose clothing and long hair (anything that could get caught in the rappel device) should be secured before attempting the rappel.

• Gloves are recommended for the rappel as the brake hand will feel friction from the rope on the descent.

- Complete the pre-climbing check.

- Visually check to see that belay set-ups are properly oriented.

- Check the knot in the end of the belay rope.

- Visually check that a locking carabiner has been properly clipped into the harness or around all the strands of the Studebaker Wrap. It should be locked and squeeze checked.

- Before climbing, check that the harness or Studebaker Wrap is belted or tied correctly according to manufacturer's recommendations.

- Make sure that the participant is wearing a correctly sized helmet and that it is put on properly.

- Follow all belay guidelines described under Best Belay Practices on page 108.

PLATFORM INSTRUCTOR'S ROLE

- It is recommended that an instructor be placed on the high platform to assist with the connection to the rappel system. As there is no transfer of belay in this situation (the belay is always on throughout the activity), a participant who has had prior training with the rappel could set up the rappel alone without an instructor present.

- After a participant climbs to the platform, the instructor then reaches out for the rappel rope. The rappel rope is usually a single length of KM3, properly knotted and attached to the pulley with a rapid link. The rappel rope is then slotted through the figure eight descender and next clipped to the participant's harness with a carabiner (next to the belay clip in).

ELEMENT SPECIFIC GUIDELINES

- Monitor the belay rope on the participant's ascent to make sure the climber follows the path of the rope.

- During the rappel, the belayer will have to feed out rope to maintain a loose belay so that the participant can descend at her own rate. Rappels should be smooth and not overly fast.

SPACE LOOPS

A series of Multi-line foot loops suspended from an overhead cable purposefully positioned to be a stretch step between each hanging rope.

SET UP
Set-up on the cable from the top down: stainless steel cable pulley, 12mm rapid link, stainless steel shear reduction device

TASK
To traverse across the element stepping from foot loop to foot loop.

FACILITATOR'S ROLE
• Complete the pre-climbing check.

• Visually check to see that belay set-ups are properly oriented.

• Check the knot in the end of the belay rope.

• Visually check that a locking carabiner has been properly clipped into the harness or around all the strands of the Studebaker Wrap. It should be locked and squeeze checked.

• Before climbing, check that the harness or Studebaker Wrap is belted or tied correctly according to manufacturer's recommendations.

• Make sure that the participant is wearing a correctly sized helmet and that it is put on properly.

• Follow all belay guidelines described under Best Belay Practices on page 108.

ELEMENT SPECIFIC GUIDELINES
• Set up the element in such a way that the belayer can move easily with the traversing participant. The belayer may give the belay rope a small amount of slack to let the climber build a loop to loop swinging momentum. Watch to make sure that the foot loops do not tangle with the belay rope.

• When lowering a participant, make sure that the climber is completely free from the hanging loops prior to the descent.

STEMMING CLIMB

A tree with naturally V-shaped trunks provides the perfect arrangement for a challenging climb between the two large supports.

SET UP
Set up on the cable from the top down: a 12mm rapid link, a stainless steel SR device.

TASK
The challenge in this activity is to climb the V slot in the naturally forked tree using any available handholds or footholds.

FACILITATOR'S ROLE
• Complete the pre-climbing check.

• Visually check to see that belay set-ups are properly oriented.

• Check the knot in the end of the belay rope.

• Visually check that a locking carabiner has been properly clipped into the harness or around all the strands of the Studebaker Wrap. It should be locked and squeeze checked.

• Before climbing, check that the harness or Studebaker Wrap is belted or tied correctly according to manufacturer's recommendations.

• Make sure that the participant is wearing a correctly sized helmet and that it is put on properly.

• Follow all belay guidelines described under Best Belay Practices in this manual.

ELEMENT SPECIFIC GUIDELINES
When lowering the climber, make sure that she keeps her hands up to gently fend off the staples and holds of the stemming climb. Lower cautiously to avoid bumping into staples.

TWO LINE BRIDGE

A foot cable is strung horizontally between trees. A second cable oriented above the first cable serves as the belay cable. In between the two is a multi-line hand cable positioned about four feet above the foot cable.

SET UP
Set up from the top down on the belay cable:
stainless steel pulley, 12mm rapid link, stainless steel SR device.

TASK
To traverse across the "bridge"— hands on the multi-line rope, feet on the bottom cable.

FACILITATOR'S ROLE
• Complete the pre-climbing check.

• Visually check to see that belay set-ups are properly oriented.

• Check the knot in the end of the belay rope.

• Visually check that a locking carabiner has been properly clipped into the harness or around all the strands of the Studebaker Wrap. It should be locked and squeeze checked.

• Before climbing, check that the harness or Studebaker Wrap is belted or tied correctly according to manufacturer's recommendations.

• Make sure that the participant is wearing a correctly sized helmet and that it is put on properly.

• Follow all belay guidelines described under Best Belay Practices in his manual.

ELEMENT SPECIFIC GUIDELINES
Set up the element in such a way that the belayer can move freely with the traversing participant.

TWO SHIPS CROSSING

This element is almost the same as a **Low Tension Traverse** except that the participants are operating at height and are starting from opposite trees with separate ropes. They meet near the middle, exchange ropes, and continue on to the opposite tree from which they started. This activity is belayed from two separate cables.

SET UP

Set up from the top down on the belay cable: stainless steel pulley, 12mm rapid link, stainless steel SR device (Install 2 sets on two separate cables).

TASK

For two people to attempt to cross the Two Ships cable from opposite sides using only Tension Traverse ropes and each other.

FACILITATOR'S ROLE

- Complete the pre-climbing check.

- Visually check to see that belay set-ups are properly oriented.

- Check the knot in the end of the belay rope.

- Visually check that a locking carabiner has been properly clipped into the harness or around all the strands of the Studebaker Wrap. It should be locked and squeeze checked.

- Before climbing, check that the harness or Studebaker Wrap is belted or tied correctly according to manufacturer's recommendations.

- Make sure that the participant is wearing a correctly sized helmet and that it is put on properly.

- Follow all belay guidelines described under Best Belay Practices in this manual.

ELEMENT SPECIFIC GUIDELINES

- Set up the element in such a way that the belayers can move easily with the traversing participant. Belayers must communicate with each other so that their belay lines to the climbers do not tangle. One belayer will pass in front of the other.

- Participants should be instructed to let go of the tension traverse rope if they fall.

- The belayer must be positioned and alert to the possibility of a pendulum fall.

- As climbers pass one another and move toward the tree, belayers should stay positioned in such a way that a fall will pull the climber away from contact with the tree.

VERTICAL PLAYPEN

Although Vertical Playpen designs vary, most include a potpourri of vertical challenges, created from rope, wooden beams and different-sized tires.

SET UP
Set up from the top down on the belay cable: 12mm rapid link, stainless steel SR device (2 sets separated by a PVC pipe).

TASK
The challenge is for two participants to help each other climb upward, over, and through a series of obstacles using balance, dexterity, and creativity.

FACILITATOR'S ROLE
- Complete the pre-climbing check.

- Visually check to see that belay set-ups are properly oriented.

- Check the knot in the end of the belay rope.

- Visually check that a locking carabiner has been properly clipped into the harness or around all the strands of the Studebaker Wrap. It should be locked and squeeze checked.

- Before climbing, check that the harness or Studebaker Wrap is belted or tied correctly according to manufacturer's recommendations.

- Make sure that the participant is wearing a correctly sized helmet and that it is put on properly.

- Follow all belay guidelines described under Best Belay Practices in this manual.

ELEMENT SPECIFIC GUIDELINES
- When mounting the start of the Vertical Playpen, have spotters spot each participant. Rope stretch at this point may prevent a belayer from arresting a ground fall.

- Do not allow participants to wrap their belay rope around horizontally suspended logs, ropes, or tires on their upward journey.

- When being lowered, instruct participants to keep hands in a bumper's up position to protect themselves from bumping into the element. It is best to lower one climber at a time.

ZIP WIRE

The Zip Wire provides an exciting means of egress from a high element. Two belays are used for the Zip. The first is a dynamic belay that runs through a large rapid link connected to a through-bolted backed-up Nut Eye located near the Zip Wire platform. The second is a static belay used for the ride down the Zip Wire. The transfer between the two occurs on the Zip Wire platform. The instructor on the Zip Wire platform oversees the transfer.

TASK
To zip down a cable on a two-wheeled cable pulley.

FACILITATOR'S ROLE
• Complete the pre-climbing check.

• Visually check to see that belay set-ups are properly oriented.

• Check the knot in the end of the belay rope.

• Visually check that a locking carabiner has been properly clipped into the harness or around all the strands of the Studebaker Wrap. It should be locked and squeeze checked.

• Before climbing, check that the harness or Studebaker Wrap is belted or tied correctly according to manufacturer's recommendations.

• Make sure that the participant is wearing a correctly sized helmet and that it is put on properly.

• Follow all belay guidelines described under Best Belay Practices in this manual.

ELEMENT SPECIFIC GUIDELINES
• One instructor is required to be on the zip platform to closely monitor the transfer of the ground belay to the zip attachment rope. (A climber must always be clipped into at least one belay). The instructor is responsible for setting up the zip pulley correctly.

• Before letting the participant zip, the instructor must check with the dismount team to make sure everyone is ready. Do a final check to ensure that the zip attachment rope is securely and correctly connected to the participant. Make sure that the participant is not still attached to the belay rope or a lobster claw.

- Have the participant move to the edge of the platform. A standing or sitting position is allowed depending upon the design of the particular element. Make sure that the participant's first step is out far enough from the platform to avoid hitting the platform edge. The exit move should be smooth and straight out from the platform. Any side to side swinging motion should be avoided.

- Most High 5 zips utilize a gravity brake system (as opposed to a bungee brake system). A dismount team needs to be in place at the take-down location to help the rider disconnect from the cable. A tall step ladder is usually used to facilitate this move.

- Care should be taken while disconnecting a rider. The supporting ladder should be spotted and the dismounting rider should descend the ladder carefully. Do not allow jumping from the ladder.

- A retrieval line is then attached to the zip pulley (if there are to be more rides) and walked back to the instructor on the platform.

- If the zip uses a bungee brake system, site specific training is recommended as the set up and operation of bungee brake systems vary.

LOW AND HIGH INDOOR ELEMENTS

Indoor Challenge Courses have become increasingly popular. Indoor sites offer several advantages over outdoor locations. These include year-round use regardless of weather, more control over unauthorized use, lower maintenance costs and more class time due to reduced travel to and from an outdoor site. Drawbacks to indoor sites may be structural limitations that preclude the installation of some elements. Examples of such limitations could be low ceiling height, type of beam configuration, and the placement of basketball hoops, lighting fixtures, bleachers, fire alarms etc. Additionally, indoor gyms are often very busy areas serving multiple purposes. Competing demands for space may limit programming opportunities. In general, though, many of the elements that have been built outdoors have now been adapted for indoor sites.

In this section are the standard operating procedures for a few elements that are for the most part used uniquely indoors. Management practices although similar to those of outside sites do require some special considerations. Elements must be able to either be stored or pulled up out of the way when not in use. Climbing holds on low traverse walls or installation hardware protruding from a wall must be either removed or covered to prevent injury from collision as well as access when unsupervised. Large ladders or lifts need to be on site to allow access to high elements in the event of an emergency.

BANGLE BOARDS

FULL HOUSE

ISLANDS

LOW SWINGING BEAM

LOW TRAVERSE WALL

BEANPOLE

CARGO NET CLIMB

FIRECRACKER LADDER

HIGH SWINGING BEAM

INCLINED MONKEY BARS

PRUSIK CLIMB

VERTICAL CLIMBING WALL

As the Bangle Boards
are constructed with
different edge surfaces,
the challenge level can be
adapted to meet the skill
level and needs of a group.

BANGLE BOARDS

Bangle Boards, a High 5 design, are free-standing 4 x 4 red cedar beams that are used in the indoor challenge course setting to simulate such classic cable elements as the Tension Traverse, the Wild Woosey and the Mohawk Walk. The Full House and TP Shuffle initiatives can also be done with Bangle Boards. The typical Bangle Board set includes: 5 ten foot beams, support cradles, and a Bangle Board carrier. Support cradles for the beams are designed to hold the beams on edge creating a narrow walking surface. Each of the 4 edge surfaces are beveled to varying degrees resulting in a range of challenges from easiest to most difficult. Ten foot beams must have 3 support cradles (two on the ends and one in the middle).

TASK(S)

Depending upon the configuration of the beams, the Bangle Boards may be used as a Tension Traverse, Wild Woosey or Mohawk Walk OR a combination of all three. SEE the Spotting Considerations under each of the elements for safety guidelines. The write-ups for the Full House and TP Shuffle are included in the Indoor Elements section. Write-ups for the others are under Low Elements.

SPOTTING CONSIDERATIONS

• The undersides of the support cradles have a rubber surface designed to protect flooring from damage. Hence, Bangle Boards may slide if there is any pressure placed against them. This may be particularly apparent in the Wild Woosey as participants traverse further out along the opening V. To keep the element from sliding, have participants stand on or place a foot against the support cradles. Added weight will keep the beams from movement.

• Spot each element configuration according to the safety guidelines listed for each element in this document.

VARIATIONS

Bangle Boards lend themselves to a variety of set-ups. Long obstacle courses can be created adding innovations from other prop activities as well. Trolleys, Stepping Stones, and/or a Nitro Swing rope can be added to the mix to create interest as well as challenge.

FULL HOUSE

SET UP
Arrange 5 Bangle boards positioned with their flat side up into the shape of a house (2 for the peaked roof, 2 for the sides and 1 for the base.

TASK
The goal of Full House is to have the group arrange themselves in a pre-scribed order on the positioned Bangle Boards without ever stepping off and touching the ground.

GUIDELINES:
• Have the participants step onto the Bangle Boards in a random order. Have them spread out so participants occupy all 5 boards.

• Tell the participants that their task is to line up in a particular order without stepping off the beams. A common directive is to get into the order of when their birthdays fall in the calendar year (month and day).

• All place exchanges must take place on the straight beams only, not at the corners. This makes the activity more challenging. Participants at the corners can help and support the people changing places.

• If a participant falls off, she must return to her original starting position. For added chal-lenge, have the whole group go back to their start point.

SPOTTING CONSIDERATIONS
• Review spotting procedures.

• Encourage participants who feel they are going to fall off to step down. Have them let go of hands so they don't pull everyone off with them.

• Use spotters as needed on the exchanges.

DEGREE OF DIFFICULTY

Basic.

A group should fit comfortably, but not necessarily easily on an island.

DEGREE OF DIFFICULTY

Basic.

ISLANDS

The Islands initiative requires the following materials: three portable platforms (two large and one small) and two doubled-up 2 x 6 boards, cut to 4 foot and 6 foot lengths respectively. The platforms should be positioned so that the boards cannot reach any of the "islands" by themselves. Place them in such a way that a combination of the boards on top of each other can cross the span.

TASK

The objective is to get the entire group from the first starting platform to the third finishing platform without touching the ground.

- Have the participants start on or behind one of the islands. Once the activity has begun, no one may touch the ground until everyone has journeyed to the last platform.

- If any member of the group touches the ground, the entire group must begin again. Modify this rule as needed depending upon the experience and age of the participants.

- If a board touches the ground, you may elect to have a penalty for this. The boards can be heavy and hard to manipulate so choose an appropriate consequence for the group's ability.

SPOTTING CONSIDERATIONS

- Explain proper lifting procedures of the boards.

- Make sure the boards are positioned securely on the platforms with a large enough overlap before an attempt is made to cross from one platform to another.

- Caution against getting fingers pinched under boards.

- Do not allow jumping off the ends of the boards onto a platform. Such movement may cause the boards to suddenly slide and fall.

VARIATIONS

If the group is large, divide them into two groups and have each group start at opposite ends. This will result in greater complexity as the groups pass each other. However, this version can be time consuming, especially for large groups. It may be preferable to have two Islands going at the same time.

LOW SWINGING BEAM

A free-swinging 4 x 4 x 16 foot laminated beam suspended on each end by a pair of overhead cables.

TASK—VARIOUS OPTIONS
- One individual mounts and walks the length of the beam, attempting to maintain her balance.
- From a distance of about two feet away from the beam, an individual attempts to step onto the beam to maintain balance for a five second count.
- To walk the beam backwards.

SPOTTING CONSIDERATIONS
The indoor swinging beam is a very dynamic element. The beam itself has both side to side and forward and back movement. As it is not that heavy, beam movement can occur quickly especially if a participant on the beam falls off suddenly. Tethers, managed by spotters, are often placed at each end of the beam to dampen sudden movement of this element.

- Spotters are placed along the beam as needed. Spotters are also used to manage the tethers. The tethers would be held loosely unless a fall occurs. Then, tension would be applied to the tethers to reduce beam movement.

- Be sure to demonstrate the potential movement of the beam if a fall occurs. Spotters should be able to adjust their spotting positions to protect both themselves and the participant when a fall occurs.

- Spotters need to be able to move laterally with the traversing participant.

- Emphasize pro-active spotting; i.e., step toward, not away from.

- Spotters must never position themselves where they can be hit by the swinging beam

- Have participants agree to not forcefully jump off the beam creating wild swinging motion.

- Have participants agree not to run on the beam.

FACILITATOR'S ROLE
Give a complete demonstration of how the beam can move and the various arcs through which it can swing.

LOW TRAVERSE WALL

A series of climbing holds selectively placed for hands and feet to create a horizontal climbing challenge. As foot holds are only 1-2 feet from the ground, protection for the climber is provided by participant spotting.

TASK

To move laterally across The Wall using the climbing holds for hand and foot placements. There are a variety of challenges that can be presented to participants. See variations for ideas.

SPOTTING CONSIDERATIONS

• Each traversing participant should have a minimum of one spotter who actively moves and spots as the climber advances.

• Traversing climbers should be prepared to step down if they become fatigued or off balance.

• Clear communication between climber and spotter are important as falls often happen quickly.

• Climbers should be directed to not climb too high on The Wall. A three foot maximum height for foot placements is recommended.

FACILITATOR'S ROLE

• The facilitator should check the climbing holds prior to the activity to make sure they are tight.

• Encourage spotters to be alert. Spotters tend to relax in this activity as the perception of risk is low as the activity is close to the ground.

GROUP SIZE

Number of participants determined by size of traverse wall.

DEGREE OF DIFFICULTY

Basic to Advanced. The challenge level may vary according to the number, configuration and placement of the holds. More holds and/or holds that are larger and easier to grip will make for an easier route. Often, routes of differing challenges can be created on the same traverse by color-coding the allowable holds for each path.

VARIATIONS

The following low wall activities were originally created by Marc Gravatt.

BALL TRAVERSE: Students traverse The Wall holding a single ball. The ball may be switched from hand to hand, but must always remain in a hand.

PICK UP: Place small beanbags on the ground at four-foot intervals along the base of The Wall. These intervals correspond with marked holds on the climbing wall. As a student traverses along The Wall, she will reach down and pick up a beanbag with one hand and place it on the marked hold. The next student who follows will remove the beanbag from the marked hold and replace it on the ground. Throwing is not allowed.

BLIND-FOLDED TRAVERSE: A partnered event between a blindfolded climber and a sighted guide. Please note that the sighted guide should not also serve as a spotter. Spotters should remain silent unless there is a safety concern.

NOTE: these are only a few of the many possible Low Traverse activities. See Bibliography for further resources.

INDOOR HIGH ELEMENTS

BEANPOLE

The Portable Pamper Pole is a unique climbing activity that combines the excitement of the traditional Pamper Pole with the benefits of a group cooperative exercise. The Pamper Pole is a free-standing stapled 16 foot 4 x 4 pole that is topped with a small wooden perch. Four ropes attached to the pole near its top are managed by spotters to help maintain an upright posture and stability for the pole. In addition, the pole is slotted into a wooden base. That too is kept in place by spotters. A traditional belay is used for the climber.

TASK

The goal of the climb is to ascend the supported pole, stand on the tiny perch, and step off the top platform. A target for the climber may be provided although a jump from the platform is not recommended as it causes too much pole movement.

SET UP AND SPECIAL SPOTTING CONSIDERATIONS

- Place the bottom of the pole in the rectangular slot in the wooden base and raise the pole to a vertical position. The pole should be positioned so that it is offset a couple of feet from the overhead belay system. This will ensure that once the climber steps from the pole, she will swing clear of the pole and its spotters. Have a minimum of two spotters support the pole to maintain placement.

- Check the knots for each of the four ropes that are slotted through the vertical pole. Stretch out the four ropes so they are at ninety degrees to one another, like the points of a compass. Assign one spotter to hold each rope.

- Have a participant prepare for climbing. See belay guidelines below.

- Once the climber is set to go, check with spotters on the pole and ropes to make sure they are ready. The rope spotters need to maintain communication throughout the climb to ensure that they are keeping the pole in a vertical position.

DEGREE OF DIFFICULTY

Advanced.
Spotters must be able
to commit fully to the
task at hand.

- As the climber begins up the pole, have additional participants spot the first few movements of the climber to not only protect the climber from a ground fall but to also protect the climber from falling into the pole spotters. A static rope could be used for the belay to reduce rope stretch.

- Once the climber is on the top, have her signal the spotters to let them know when she is stepping from the platform. Often, however, falls from this perch happen quickly so spotters must be prepared for pole movement.

FACILITATOR'S ROLE

- Complete the pre-climbing check.

- Check the knot in the end of the belay rope.

- Visually check that a locking carabiner has been clipped into the harness or around all the strands of the Studebaker Wrap. It should be locked and squeeze checked.

- Before climbing, check that the harness or Studebaker Wrap is tied or belted correctly according to manufacturer's recommendations.

- Make sure that the participant is wearing a correctly sized helmet and that it is put on properly.

- Follow all belay guidelines described under Best Belay Practices on page 108.

ELEMENT SPECIFIC GUIDELINES

The belayer must make sure that the climber follows a direct path up the pole to avoid rope wrap on the pole.

CARGO NET CLIMB (VERTICAL PLACEMENT)

**The Cargo Net is a large rectangular net fashioned from 5/8"
Multi-line rope that is woven into approximately one foot square
blocks. Hung vertically, a participant climbs the rope blocks in a
ladder-like technique.**

TASK

The challenge is to ascend as high as possible on the Cargo Net. If
desired, spotters placed at the bottom of the Net may hold the element
steady to reduce side to side movement.

FACILITATOR'S ROLE

• Complete the pre-climbing check.

• Check the knot in the end of the belay rope.

• Visually check that a locking carabiner has been clipped into the harness or around all the strands of the Studebaker Wrap. It should be
locked and squeeze checked.

• Before climbing, check that the harness or Studebaker Wrap is tied or
belted correctly according to manufacturer's recommendations.

• Make sure that the participant is wearing a correctly sized helmet and
that it is put on properly.

• Follow all belay guidelines described under Best Belay Practices on
page 108.

ELEMENT SPECIFIC GUIDELINES

• Advise climbers to not poke their heads through the Cargo Net holes
while climbing as the shifting tensions in the rope squares could cause
constriction of the openings.

• When lowering a climber, have a participant pull the Cargo Net to the
side, clear of the descent.

**DEGREE OF
DIFFICULTY**

Basic to Intermediate

FIRECRACKER LADDER

Advanced.

The Firecracker ladder is a free hanging ladder-like climb that can provide exciting access to other high elements or operate as a separate element. The Firecracker Ladder is uniquely constructed of hardwood rungs that are secured at their middle to a central climbing line. Given the features of this design, the firecracker ladder becomes a challenging event requiring good technique and persistence.

TASK
The challenge is to climb the swaying element. The climb may be made easier by having a spotter hold the base of the apparatus.

FACILITATOR'S ROLE
- Complete the pre-climbing check.

- Check the knot in the end of the belay rope.

- Visually check that a locking carabiner has been clipped into the harness or around all the strands of the Studebaker Wrap. It should be locked and squeeze checked.

- Before climbing, check that the harness or Studebaker Wrap is tied or belted correctly according to manufacturer's recommendations.

- Make sure that the participant is wearing a correctly sized helmet and that it is put on properly.

- Follow all belay guidelines described under Best Belay Practices in this manual.

ELEMENT SPECIFIC GUIDELINES
- The belayer must monitor the climber closely to make sure she follows the path of the belay rope to avoid wraps and twists around the Firecracker Ladder.

- It is recommended that a spotter holding the base of the Firecracker Ladder for a climber wear a helmet.

- When lowering a climber, have a participant pull the ladder to the side, clear of the descending climber.

HIGH SWINGING BEAM

The High Swinging Beam is a 4' x 4' x 16' free-swinging laminated beam horizontally suspended from overhead cables.

TASK
To climb to the beam via a rope ladder and attempt to cross from one end of the beam to the other.

FACILITATOR'S ROLE
- Complete the pre-climbing check.

- Check the knot in the end of the belay rope.

- Visually check that a locking carabiner has been clipped into the harness or around all the strands of the Studebaker Wrap. It should be locked and squeeze checked.

- Before climbing, check that the harness or Studebaker Wrap is tied or belted correctly according to manufacturer's recommendations.

- Make sure that the participant is wearing a correctly sized helmet and that it is put on properly.

- Follow all belay guidelines described under Best Belay Practices in this manual.

ELEMENT SPECIFIC GUIDELINES
- Belayers should monitor the tautness of the belay rope carefully. As the Swinging Beam moves freely and easily, climbers often hold onto their belay ropes tightly for added security. Make sure that no slack builds up in the belay as the climber makes her crossing. However, as the overhead belay cable is intentionally slightly offset from the beam to allow falls to be directed away from the beam, too much tension in the belay will pull the climber off balance.

- Lowering the climber off the beam should be done slowly and smoothly to prevent contact with the beam. Do not allow jumping from the element.

DEGREE OF DIFFICULTY

Intermediate

INCLINED MONKEY BARS

The Inclined Monkey Bars features an aluminum ladder suspended horizontally from the ceiling of the gym. The ladder is set at a slight angle with the lowest rung at the access point. Participants climb a rope ladder to get to the first rung.

Advanced.

TASK
The challenge is for the climber to reach the inclined ladder and move hand over hand along the ladder as far as possible.

FACILITATOR'S ROLE
- Complete the pre-climbing check.

- Check the knot in the end of the belay rope.

- Visually check that a locking carabiner has been clipped into the harness or around all the strands of the Studebaker Wrap. It should be locked and squeeze checked.

- Before climbing, check that the harness or Studebaker Wrap is tied or belted correctly according to manufacturer's recommendations.

- Make sure that the participant is wearing a correctly sized helmet and that it is put on properly.

- Follow all belay guidelines described under Best Belay Practices on page 108.

ELEMENT SPECIFIC GUIDELINES
- A back clip on this event is preferred as it keeps the belay rope out of the way of the face of the climber. A chest harness is strongly recommended. This should be correctly fitted to the participant and connected to the seat harness and rope properly.

- Set up the element in such a way that the belayer can move easily with the traversing participant. The belayer may let out a small amount of slack in the belay rope to allow the climber to have enough rope to move easily from rung to rung.

PRUSIK CLIMBS

A vertically hung length of Multi-line rope that is outfitted with two or three sets of prusik slings: the highest to be clipped into the climbing harness, the lower one or two to be used for foot placements.

TASK

To climb the hanging Multi-line rope with the aid of the two or three prusik slings. Progress is attained by moving each of the Prusik loops upward in a rhythmic sequenced motion. As the Prusik knot tightens and grabs when weighted, any upward gain is maintained when the climber's weight is applied to the knot. Rest stops therefore can be taken at any point on the climb. For backup protection, the climb is belayed.

FACILITATOR'S ROLE

• Complete the pre-climbing check.

• Check the knot in the end of the belay rope.

• Visually check that a locking carabiner has been clipped into the harness or around all the strands of the Studebaker Wrap. It should be locked and squeeze checked.

• Before climbing, check that the harness or Studebaker Wrap is tied or belted correctly according to manufacturer's recommendations.

• Make sure that the participant is wearing a correctly sized helmet and that it is put on properly.

• Follow all belay guidelines described under Best Belay Practices on page 108.

ELEMENT SPECIFIC GUIDELINES

• This element may be made somewhat easier if a spotter weights the Multi-line rope.

• The belayer must make sure that the belay line does not get wrapped around the Prusik climb.

• A participant may down climb the element by reversing the motion of the Prusiks or she may be lowered on the belay rope. To lower, all Prusiks should be first loosened and unweighted. On the descent, the climber needs to hold above the top prusik to help slide the loops down the rope.

DEGREE OF DIFFICULTY

Basic to Intermediate
A certain amount of coordination and strength is needed to effectively operate the Prusik loops.

VERTICAL CLIMBING WALL

The climbing wall features a vertical arrangement of various climbing holds sequenced to create a climbing route or routes. Additional features such as overhangs and friction slabs may be constructed if the climbing wall is built of plywood. Often, a platform mounted on The Wall serves as a target destination. The lower climbing holds may be removed to prevent unwanted access to The Wall. An alternative system to reduce access is to conceal the lower holds during periods of non-use with a secured curtain or covering.

TASK
To climb using the various holds for hand and foot placements.

FACILITATOR'S ROLE
- Complete the pre-climbing check.

- Check the knot in the end of the belay rope.

- Visually check that a locking carabiner has been clipped into the harness or around all the strands of the Studebaker Wrap. It should be locked and squeeze checked.

- Before climbing, check that the harness or Studebaker Wrap is tied or belted correctly according to manufacturer's recommendations.

- Make sure that the participant is wearing a correctly sized helmet and that it is put on properly.

- Follow all belay guidelines described under Best Belay Practices on page 108.

ELEMENT SPECIFIC GUIDELINES
- If the belay is a fixed point, make sure the climber follows a route that is more or less vertically below the anchor point. Too much lateral movement would widen the angle from the belay and could result in a pendulum fall.

- Check climbing holds on a regular basis to make sure they are tight.

DEGREE OF DIFFICULTY

The challenge level of climbing wall routes can be easily altered by changing the number, placement and size of the climbing holds.

APPENDICES

APPENDIX A

THINKING PRACTITIONER RESPONSES

Note: The thoughts expressed regarding the Thinking Practitioner Questions below are from our perspective as an educational organization and as practitioners who are passionate about adventure education. We believe adventure learning is a powerful tool for education and our thoughts on programming are shaped by this principle.

All of these questions are based upon questions that have been asked of us and situations that have actually occurred.

CAUGHT YOU THINKING #1:

Our school just got $12,000 to build a climbing wall, can you help us?

Sure, make the check out to…! This is actually a fun question to receive and it actually comes into the High 5 office quite regularly. The fun part is responding in such a way that genuinely convinces the caller that we are not after their money but more interested in helping them develop their program thoughtfully. Our standard response is, "Tell us about your program; what are you trying to accomplish by building the wall?" This usually leads to an exploratory discussion about *all* the ways they can implement an adventure education program at their site and also all the ways in which they can spend their $12,000.

Now this is an intriguing question. Coming from an adventure education program background this has all the markings of an amusement park approach that is focused on numbers only. The compelling question might logically be, "Why do you need to get 45 or even 30 people through the course in an hour?" This is a classic question to stimulate a discussion about what adventure education is all about. From a High 5 perspective it is not about how many people you can crank through the course in an hour but the quality of the experience and the learning that takes place.

This particular situation involved a summer camp trying to provide an adventure experience for their campers. The staff person asking this question was in a quandary and rightly so given that his approach to providing a meaningful adventure experience was being tested by the demand for greater numbers. Another discussion on this question could involve the safety implications of such an approach.

Obviously, every organization needs to make their numbers work. The question is "how." There are countless ways to increase revenue some of which may or not fit well with an organization's direction and purpose. In this instance, the challenge with the marketing consultant's plan was that his focus was not about developing the existing programs, it was more about the 15–20% increase in revenues. The organization that he was advising did not currently offer corporate-type programs given that their focus was more with camps and schools. In addition to creating a bit of a conflict regarding the organization's purpose and direction, taking on this kind of work with staff trained primarily for camp and school clientele can prove problematic as they attempt to work successfully within a corporate venue.

CAUGHT YOU THINKING #2:

My director just asked me to increase the number of people I can get through the challenge course from 30 to 45 people per hour. What should I do?

CAUGHT YOU THINKING #3:

Our director hired a marketing consultant to help us increase revenues 15–20% over the next three to five years. He recommended a heavy focus on bringing in corporate programs for teambuilding days.

CAUGHT YOU THINKING #4:

I'd like to bring 35 eighth graders for a day of challenge course activities. We'll arrive at 9 am and need to leave by 2 pm. We'd like to have everybody do at least one high element. Our budget is limited, so I thought perhaps some of our teachers could help belay. Please get back to me as soon as possible.

There are several different issues in this question. First, assume that the program goal of having everyone do at least one high element makes sense (appropriate lead up activities have been completed at their site) and that they are coming to the course specifically to experience high challenge course opportunities. So the issue in question is whether we should use their teachers as belayers.

SOME THOUGHTS: Are these people trained belayers? If yes, where were they trained? How much time was spent instructing them? How much practice have they had? When was the last time they belayed? Are these staff with whom you are familiar? If they are not trained belayers, is the expectation that you will train these people the day of the program?

If you are considering using people in this capacity, it is recommended that they have received training by a skilled instructor to the same degree that a person would have received those skills in a professional training workshop, i.e., ground school, one to two days pf practice, etc. They should be current in their skills, meaning they have used their skills in the past twelve months on more than one occasion. However, even if they meet all of these criteria, if you do not know these people prior this program day then you are agreeing to have unknown people serve as belayers in your program. This is problematic for many reasons, not the least of which is your insurance may not cover the actions of such individuals should an accident occur.

In summary, agreeing to such a plan is not generally a good idea unless you have trained the individuals or have seen credentials attesting to their skills, are personally comfortable with their skill level and are sure they will be covered by your insurance.

If the assumption mentioned previously was true, that the hope was that these teachers could be trained the day of the program, the answer is much simpler, "don't do it."

Note: The use of the Australian belay would provide a simple solution provided the elements being chosen are suitable for such a technique.

These are two classic questions. The quick answers are, you need a lot of training and you can never know too much. However, the first sounds like a sales pitch and the second is a cliché that does not really give you an answer.

To be more serious, it is generally a sound idea to match the necessary training skills to the level of program you are facilitating. For example:

PROGRAM	RECOMMENDED TRAINING DAYS
Games & Initiatives Only	1–2
Games & Initiatives & Low Challenge Elements	2–3
Games, Initiatives Lows & Highs	4–5
Advanced level skills training for High Elements	4–5
Program Management Training for Challenge Course	3

These are estimates of training time based upon average workshop lengths offered by a variety of vendors in the field. These are minimum training times to prepare someone adequately in the various skill sets associated with the competencies required for each category.

Like any profession, ongoing training is the key to keeping skills current. Ongoing implies that there are not long periods of inactivity in one's training path. We recommend that practitioners participate in some training annually and that they attend a formal training every three years.

CAUGHT YOU THINKING #5:

How much training do I need? How do I know if I know enough?

CAUGHT YOU THINKING #6

A GriGri belay device makes belaying safer.

This is an overly simple statement that is frequently applied to this piece of equipment. We have encountered countless practitioners and program managers over the years that make this claim. Their logic is somewhat understandable because they have been told that a GriGri will automatically arrest a fall if the belayer takes their brake hand off the rope, i.e., loses control of the climber's descent. This is true; a GriGri has a camming action that will do just that. The problem sometimes lies in the next step of the process which requires the belayer to lower the climber to the ground. To do so requires that the lever on the GriGri be released slowly as the belayer begins to use a standard belay technique in conjunction with the device. For the trained belayer, this is an easily accomplished task. However, it is at this point that the unskilled belayer can lose control by lifting the lever too quickly or too far. We are familiar with several incidents where this has taken place.

So the quick answer is that a GriGri does not necessarily make belaying safer. It is a fine device when used properly but properly implies that it is being used by a facilitator who is trained in appropriate belay techniques and is familiar with the GriGri.

CAUGHT YOU THINKING #7

What is a Nut Eye Bolt? Do I need to know?

Having some of knowledge about the equipment used to construct a challenge course is never a bad idea. However, the typical practitioner does not need to know the name and application of each and every piece of hardware. A useful guideline for information in this regard can be found in Section 2 under the heading Challenge Course Inspection & Equipment Tips. These are tips for practitioners to put into practice at their sites. Obviously one needs adequate knowledge of the equipment referenced to be able to use the gear with a degree of quality. For example, it would be difficult to check the tightness of cable clamps if you did not know what a cable clamp looks like. On the other hand knowing whether a nut eye bolt or a thimble eye bolt should be used for a specific application is really the responsibility of a challenge course builder, not the practitioner.

Reference to this Thinking Practitioner scenario was made on pg. 26 under the heading, Participant Readiness—Informed Consent. The focus of that explanation had to do with the responsibility of programs to inform participants of what they can expect should they be involved with adventure education programs and challenge course activities. That explanation is repeated below in its entirety. We would also add that, in addition to Participant Readiness—Informed Consent issues, the main point to be made here is simply that inappropriate or out of context use of adventure activities can be unsafe physically and emotionally and that activities such as these are best part of an established adventure education program.

The scenario from pg. 26 is repeated below:

Some years ago a ten-year-old girl was attending a week-long session at a summer camp. When she returned home she was asked how she had enjoyed her week. She gave a somewhat standard response indicating that it was a lot of fun. She went on to say that they even did a little adventure stuff. Her parent inquired about the type of activities and she replied that they did trust falls. Her parent pursued the questioning by asking how it went. Her response was "Not good, they dropped the first two people!" The parent was slightly shocked. The girl continued by saying, "Don't worry, I was number three and we stopped at two."

This situation has always reminded me that people, in this instance, the girl and her parents, need to know what to expect from a program. Further information about the situation revealed that this particular camp was not an adventure camp and, in fact, made no reference to any adventure activities in their literature. However, during the week of staff training (general training not adventure training), prior to the beginning of camp, a number of adventure teambuilding activities were done with the staff. Trust falls was one of them. It turns out that the staff member that led the trust falls with the campers was merely trying to fill some free time utilizing the activity she had experienced during her staff orientation.

CAUGHT YOU THINKING #8

We did trust falls at camp today. How did it go? Not good, they dropped the first two people!

CAUGHT YOU THINKING #9

Can you train twenty of my staff to run the Zip Wire for our summer camp? I have about two hours available during our week-long staff training period!

Obviously the answer to this one is pretty straightforward, "No!"

There is really not a part of this question that is not out of synch with commonly held best practices in the field regarding the training of staff as adventure practitioners. A plan to train that many staff to run any element, particularly a specialty element like the Zip Wire, is simply not wise.

In this instance, the camp making the request was trying to have each group leader be versed in running the Zip Wire so they could stay with their group as they did their challenge course experience. The logic of the request was steeped in the program structure of the camp, not in the prevailing logic of how to run a challenge course with well-trained staff. Providing only a two-hour time slot in the midst of other staff training is another indicator of a lack of understanding of what it takes to run an adventure based program.

Programs need professional guidance to develop sound practices. The letter on page 15 is our attempt to help programs develop such practices and to provide a clear understanding of the complexities and challenges involved in running safe and successful challenge course programs.

CAUGHT YOU THINKING #10

We'd like to bring our students for a day on your challenge course. We're only interested in the high elements.

This type of statement is a red flag for us at High 5. Often it is an indicator that the group is looking for a thrill experience, as opposed to an educational one. It may or not be something we want to provide given our approach to adventure learning. Other times, we discover as we ask further questions that this is simply a customer who needs more information about the available programming options. Generally sending them our Program Goals Form (see the Appendix) will help them formulate their thoughts regarding their goals and allow us to structure a program that will meet their needs.

It also quite possible that a group requesting just a high challenge course experience is doing so because they have done their own games, initiatives, trust activities and low elements at their site and are looking specifically for a high element experience to round out their program. If this is the case then such a day fits well into a logical program sequence and makes sense.

Of course every program must decide for themselves what type of experiences they are willing to provide. We find that the one-day, high-only experience without prior experience and opportunities for group development can lead to less participation, unnecessary anxiety, limited group interaction and therefore a less than beneficial experience for those involved.

Here are a few responses from our High 5 training staff:

- *One that I particularly like is **Gotcha**. This warm-up seems to work well for most any group from youth to corporate. I like it for several reasons. It allows the group to be in a circle, which is always a good beginning since a circle allows for eye contact, easy communication etc. It also requires very little commitment on the part of participants to be involved. As a start-up activity for someone who might be suspicious or reluctant of what the day ahead holds, it seems to easily engage participants and quickly bring a smile and some laughter to the group. These are two things that always make for a good beginning.*
(Jim Grout)

- *I really like to use the game **Name Roulette** as one of my openers. If participants do not know each other, I usually do another name game first or something that will at least familiarize members of the group with each other. **Name Roulette** has been a stand-out activity for me as it sets the right tone for the ensuing workshop. It has a good tempo with movement, laughter and energy. It sets a slight edge with its competitive team challenge, but simultaneously makes it OK to make errors and be confused. Participants are usually full of energy after the activity and are ready to dive into a more substantial challenge.*
(Nicki Hall)

- *I like using **Object or Postcard Introductions** as a starter. I think it works particularly well because often people are arriving at slightly different times and it gives them something to do during that "awkward" period before the workshop starts. It is also a conversation starter. People are more comfortable having an object to which they can attach their thoughts and feelings. Then being asked to share with just one person at first helps them maximize their comfort level. This activity is a sure winner for getting a group to interact and learn about one another.*
(Jen Stanchfield)

- *When I am just starting up the day with a group, I am trying to do two things; get to know my group and have some light-hearted fun. **Bumpity-Bump-Bump** is the game for me in this situation. While it can be confusing to connect names with faces in this fast paced name game, I do get to hear everyone's name repeated ad nauseam. On top of that, forgetting your own name or just trying to say **Bumpity-Bump-Bump** never fails to get a giggle.*
(Chris Ortiz)

CAUGHT YOU THINKING #11

What's your favorite opening game for groups? Why does it work?

CAUGHT YOU THINKING #12

Has it become common practice for adventure programs to have participants wear climbing helmets while doing the 12' Initiative Wall?

The quick answer is "no." You occasionally hear about programs that have decided to do this as part of their local operating procedures, but such a practice is not commonplace at this time. Yet such a practice even in its limited use is worthy of analysis.

Questions one might ask are:

• Do helmets increase the safety of the participants?

• What purpose would they serve in the event of a fall? Is it possible that they could in fact decrease the safety of participants if grabbed by a lifter on the top of the wall when trying to assist someone coming up?

• Could a loose-fitting helmet actually become a hazard for a participant in the process of climbing the wall (i.e., if a loose chin strap resulted in the helmet falling off one's head and the chin strap settled upon the neck area)?

• Could they become a hazard for spotters and lifters if a climber were to slip or fall onto the group?

Before implementing such a practice at one's site, it is important to thoughtfully weigh the pros and cons.

CAUGHT YOU THINKING #13

True or False? The use of the body belay is a dated practice that should not be used in most programs.

The formal name for this technique is the standing hip belay and while it certainly is used less frequently than some years ago it is still an accepted practice. Belay devices have become the norm for most challenge course programs in the field. Some typical choices are Stitch plates, Black Diamond Air Traffic Controllers (ATCs), Trango pyramids, etc. Yet High 5 feels that it is still a good practice to have participants become familiar with the standing hip belay. It is a useful technique for the back-up belayer and in the event of an emergency can allow a belayer to get into a belay position quickly.

This question is a good example of a practice that is still safe but has become unfamiliar to some practitioners.

The short answer is that either practice is acceptable. This is really a local operating procedure decision. One rationale you hear for using two is that if one screw gate gets left open then there is a second carabiner to serve as a back-up. A counter rationale for using just one is that simple is better. The thought here is that using less equipment requires fewer procedural steps thereby lessening the possibility of errors.

This is one of those issues that warrant monitoring the trend in the field. As with so many practices norms change over time and staying current with best practices is always recommended.

CAUGHT YOU THINKING #14

I've heard that two carabiners should be used to clip climbers into the belay rope. Our program uses one. Which method is correct?

APPENDIX B:

GLOSSARY OF TERMS

ACCT—Association for Challenge Course Technology, an international association of challenge course vendors and practitioners who meet regularly to establish safe building and operational standards for the challenge course field. (www. acctinfo.org)

The Association for Challenge Course Technology was incorporated in 1993 after a series of symposia held by a group of challenge course vendors. This group saw an increasing need for installation and inspection standards in the challenge course industry. Representatives from several professional challenge course vendors created the first edition of the ACCT standards which were published in 1994, containing standards for installation and inspection. The intent of these standards was to produce a document that represented a common voice for professionals and practitioners outlining minimum strength standards for challenge course installations. At the same time, the Installations Standards Committee wanted to preserve enough flexibility in the document to allow for individual vendor creativity and variances in design and building practices.

ACCT later developed the Operations Standards, to more fully recognize the importance of training and facilitator competencies in the effective use of the challenge course.

BELAY—A technique with rope that is used to protect a climber.

BELAY DEVICES—Devices that use friction on the rope to control and slow a faller's descent; these include: Stitch plate, Trango pyramid, Black Diamond ATC, GriGri and several others.

BOWLINE ON A BIGHT—A popular knot for tying on the end of the belay rope; displays a high tensile strength and has the capability of easily releasing after having sustained a shock load.

BRAKE HAND—A belayer's dominant hand, used to stop or slow the movement of rope through a belay device or around a belayer's body (in the case of a standing hip belay).

CARABINER—A strong connecting device made of steel or alloy that has many purposes on a challenge course. One primary use is to connect the climber to the belay rope.

CHALLENGE BY CHOICE—The choice offered to participants that allows them to choose their level of participation and challenge in an impending activity. (Project Adventure, Inc.)

DYNAMIC BELAY—A means of protecting a climber with rope, where the rope is controlled by another person. (See **Static Belay**.)

EXPERIENTIAL LEARNING CYCLE—A theoretical concept developed by David Kolb and Richard Fry in 1975 that highlights four phases of a learning cycle: concrete experience, reflective observation, abstract conceptualization and active experimentation.

FIGURE 8 DEVICE—A device frequently used for rappelling (see Rappel) i.e., sliding down a single or double rope from height in a controlled manner; also called abseil.

DOUBLE FIGURE 8—The knot most used by High 5 to provide a secure loop in the end of a climbing rope. This double-rope loop is clipped, using a locking carabiner into the climber's harness.

FULL VALUE AGREEMENT—An agreement between participants (including the facilitator) that establishes group behavior norms.

HAWSER-LAY ROPE—Rope that is twisted together in three strands; multi-line is an example of hawser-lay rope; easy to splice.

HAUL CORD—#4 nylon cord used for hauling a belay rope up and through a shear reduction device or rapid link. Use of the cord precludes having to climb and reeve the cord through the Shear Reduction belay device.

KERNMANTLE—Generic name for climbing rope; *kern* represents the rope's interior: parallel nylon fibers that extend the length of the rope; *mantle* is the woven exterior, usually brightly hued

MULTI-LINE—A durable, twisted, three-strand rope (usually white) made of polyester with a colored polypropylene tracer; easily spliced.

NEB—NUT EYE BOLT—A very strong, drop forged bolt used extensively in challenge course construction.

RAPPEL—(French) The procedure for sliding down a single or double rope using an attached friction device; also called *abseil* (German).

REEVE—To pass or thread (as the end of a rope) through a hole or opening.

RETIRED ROPE—Rope that is no longer used where safety is a concern.

SAFE WORKING LOAD—One-fifth, or 20%, of the average tensile strength of rope, eyebolts, carabiners (See **Tensile Strength**.)

SELF-BELAY SYSTEMS—A single-person belay system that requires energy-absorbing commercial lanyards to meet current safety standards.

SHEAR—The severe stretch applied to rope fibers as they pass, under load, over a small-diameter object (carabiner); shear weakens rope substantially.

SHEAR REDUCTION DEVICE—A shear reduction device (SRD) is a piece of hardware that is often part of a belay set-up. Its purpose is to extend the life of a climbing rope by having the rope pass over its relatively wide surface. The SRD helps to reduce shear and to maintain a higher proportion of the rope's breaking strength. The ACCT Standard B7.[1] requires that a belay rope "turn over a fitting with a minimum of 12mm."

SPLICE—Manipulation of the three strands in hawser lay rope that allows a strong connection between two ends of rope; includes forming an eye in the end of a rope.

SPOTTING—A technique used to physically protect the upper part of a participant's body in the event of a low/slow fall. Spotting is primarily used on low challenge course elements. (See **Belay**.)

STANDING END—The end of the rope not actively used in tying a knot. (See **Working End**.)

STATIC BELAY—A rope or self-belay lanyard that protects a climber by connecting directly to an object or belay cable, not to another person (belayer). An example of a static belay is the special lanyard or tether used to protect a participant during the Zip Wire ride.

STUDEBAKER WRAP—A self-tied harness arrangement that is essentially a Swiss Seat tied fore and aft; allows front and rear clip in; less comfortable than a commercial harness, but also less expensive.

TENSILE STRENGTH—The actual breaking strength of an object (rope, bolt, etc.) determined by a destructive testing procedure; a theoretical figure in the case of rope because rope cannot be broken in a destructive testing scenario without knots having been tied in the rope.

UNIVERSAL HARNESS—The brand name of a commonly used harness on challenge courses manufactured by Climb High. It has both a front and a rear clip-in.

UIAA—Union of the International Alpine Association— Internationally recognized organization that sets standards for climbing and mountaineering equipment.

U/V—Ultraviolet sun rays; climbing ropes are susceptible to and degraded by U/V rays.

WORKING END—The end of the rope used in tying a knot. (See **Standing End**.)

1 Challenge Course Standards 6th Edition – The Association for Challenge Course Technology, 2004

APPENDIX C:

FORMS

PROGRAM DEVELOPMENT

130 Austine Drive
Brattleboro, VT 05301
802-254-8718/
802-251-7203 fax
www.high5adventure.org

Whether you are beginning a new program or expanding an existing one, your answers to the questions below will help us to guide you in the development of your adventure education program. Answer each question as thoroughly as possible and call us if you have any questions or need to discuss specific items with us. Feel free to use the reverse side if more space is needed. Thank you!

CONTACT PERSON   **SITE NAME**

PROGRAM INTEGRATION:

What are your overarching goals for your adventure program? Do you have any particular target goals for specific populations? How will the adventure program be incorporated into your organization? (i.e. part of a school physical education curriculum / classroom based / summer camp activity, etc.)

_____

_____

_____

_____

_____

PARTICIPANTS:

What size are your groups? How frequently do they meet? What age group do you work with?

_____

_____

_____

BUDGET:

Is there an established budget for developing/maintaining your program? (i.e. staff training, equipment purchases, challenge course constructions, etc.)

_____

_____

_____

NEXT STEPS:

Do you have any time lines/deadlines for receiving a proposal from High 5?

_____

_____

PROGRAM GOALS INFORMATION[1]

130 Austine Drive
Brattleboro, VT 05301
802-254-8718/
802-251-7203 fax
www.high5adventure.org

Adventure
Learning Center

The more we know about your group, the better equipped we will be to design a program that matches your group's goals and expectations for the High 5 experience. Please be specific when filling out this form. Feel free to use the reverse side if more space is needed.

CONTACT PERSON

GROUP NAME

NUMBER OF PARTICIPANTS

PROGRAM DATES

BACKGROUND:
Please tell us about your group. How long has the group been together? What dynamics exist within the group that may have an impact on its experience?

PRIOR EXPERIENCE:
Please describe any teambuilding or experiential activities this group may have done prior to this workshop.

GOALS:
What do you wish to accomplish with your group via an adventure experience? Topics might include: communication, team-building, empowerment, problem solving, among others.

SPECIAL REQUESTS:
Please explain any special requests or needs your group may have.

NEXT STEPS:
How does your organization plan to follow up on this experience?

APPLICANT CONFIDENTIAL INFORMATION, ASSUMPTION OF RISKS, AND AGREEMENTS OF RELEASE AND INDEMNITY

130 Austine Drive
Brattleboro, VT 05301
802-254-8718/
802-251-7203 fax
www.high5adventure.org

To All Participants in the High 5 Program: Welcome to High 5! Please read this document carefully. It provides important information about your High 5 experience. If you have any questions please call us.

High 5 Adventure Learning Center (High 5) is a non profit educational organization. High 5 Programs are designed for those in reasonably good health and incorporate a variety of activities, including games and initiatives and more strenuous low and high challenge course elements. The activities may be conducted on the ground or at heights of up to fifty feet, indoors and out. Certain activities may involve close personal contact with other persons. Participants must follow the instructions of the High 5 staff. Each participant may choose the level of his or her participation, recognizing that there is a risk of harm even though minimizing risks is a high priority at High 5. Injuries and other losses can result from, among other causes, moderate to strenuous activity, the possibility of falling, or abrupt contact with other participants, staff, or structures associated with the activity. The outcomes of such risks may include, among others, sprains, breaks, abrasions and other trauma, some of which may be serious. High 5 recommends that participants be covered by health and accident insurance during the time of their participation.

Please complete the following questionnaire prior to your participation. This information will be used to inform staff of any pre-existing medical condition and determine if consultation with your physician seems prudent prior to your participation.

PART I - GENERAL HISTORY

NAME _____ DATE OF BIRTH _____ SEX: MALE ? FEMALE

ADDRESS _____

NAME OF INSURANCE CARRIER _____

APPLICANT CONFIDENTIAL INFORMATION, ASSUMPTION OF RISKS, AND AGREEMENTS OF RELEASE AND INDEMNITY, CONTINUED

PART II-MEDICAL INFORMATION

Do you have any disabilities (temporary or permanent) that you or your doctor feel would limit your participation in High 5's programs?　　○ Yes　○ No

If you answered Yes, please explain:

_____

_____

_____

_____

Please list any medications you are currently taking and the conditions they are treating.

_____

_____

_____

_____

Do you have allergies?　○ Yes　○ No

Reactions to medications?　○ Yes　○ No

Other medical limitations?　○ Yes　○ No

If you answered Yes to any part of this question, please explain:

_____

_____

_____

_____

PART III - MEDICAL HISTORY

Have you had surgery in the past year for any conditions that might limit your participation?　○ Yes　○ No

Are you under follow-up surgical care?　○ Yes　○ No

If you answered Yes to any part of this question, please explain:

_____

_____

_____

APPLICANT CONFIDENTIAL INFORMATION, ASSUMPTION OF RISKS, AND AGREEMENTS OF RELEASE AND INDEMNITY, CONTINUED

Do you currently have, or have you a history of any of the following?

Chest Pain	◯ Yes ◯ No		High Blood Pressure	◯ Yes ◯ No
Heart Attack	◯ Yes ◯ No		Heart Disease	◯ Yes ◯ No
Heart Murmur	◯ Yes ◯ No		Heart Palpitations	◯ Yes ◯ No
Stroke	◯ Yes ◯ No			

When you exert yourself, do you experience symptoms of any of the above?   ◯ Yes   ◯ No

If you answered Yes to any part of the last question, please provide details:

_____

_____

ADDITIONAL INFORMATION

If you answered Yes to any part of the Medical History questions above, High 5 strongly recommends that you see a physician before participation.

Do you have diabetes?   ◯ Yes   ◯ No

If you answered Yes, are you dependent on insulin?   ◯ Yes   ◯ No

Is there a history of heart disease in your family?   ◯ Yes   ◯ No

If you answered yes, please elaborate:

_____

Do you smoke?   ◯ Yes   ◯ No

Are you a former smoker?   ◯ Yes   ◯ No

If you answered Yes, when did you stop?

_____

How often do you exercise?   ◯ No regular exercise   ◯ 1-2 times/week   ◯ 3+ times/week

If you have a number of the following cardiac risk factors, High 5 strongly recommends that you consult your physician before participation: lead a sedentary lifestyle, smoke, are overweight, have diabetes, are 45 years of age or have a family history of heart disease. If you or your physician would like more information regarding the activities included in your program, please contact High 5.

I have consulted my physician: ◯

My physician advises me that I may participate fully.   ◯

My physician has advised me to avoid certain activities.   ◯

My physician advised me not to participate.   ◯

If your physician has limited or disapproved your participation, please provide further details:

_____

_____

In the event of injury or illness, please contact:

_____

NAME   **RELATIONSHIP**

_____

ADDRESS

_____

DAYTIME PHONE   **EVENING PHONE**

I understand that failure to answer this questionnaire in a full and comprehensive manner could affect my own safety as well as that of others, and therefore I affirm that the information herein is accurate and complete. I agree to hold High 5 Learning Center harmless if full disclosure of a pre-existing medical condition has not been made.

···

PART IV-ASSUMPTION OF RISKS, AND AGREEMENTS OF RELEASE AND INDEMNITY

In consideration of the services of High 5, I agree as follows:

Assumption of Risks: I acknowledge that I understand the activities in which I will be participating, and their risks. I understand that the risks are inherent in the activities-that is, they cannot be eliminated without changing the nature and value of the experience. I voluntarily assume all such risks, inherent and otherwise, and whether or not they are described above.

Release and Indemnity: I hereby release and agree to indemnify (that is, defend and pay any judgments, including costs and attorneys fees) High 5 Adventure Learning Center, Inc., its owners, staff members and Board of Directors ("Released Parties") from any and all claims and liabilities arising from an injury or other loss suffered by me related in whole or part to my enrollment or participation in High 5 activities. These agreements of release and indemnity include claims of negligence, but not claims of recklessness or willful misconduct.

Other: In the event of illness or injury, consent is hereby given to provide emergency medical care, hospitalization or other treatment, which may become necessary. If a suite is filed against High 5 or any other released party it must be filed in the County of Windham State of Vermont. Any such suit will be governed by the laws of the State of Vermont, not including those laws which may apply the laws of another jurisdiction. I hereby grant High 5 permission to use, reproduce, or distribute any photographs, films, videotapes and/or sound recordings of me during my training for use in materials it may create, for marketing or other purposes.

STUDENT PROGRAM INFORMATION, ASSUMPTION OF RISKS AND AGREEMENTS OF RELEASE AND INDEMNITY

130 Austine Drive
Brattleboro, VT 05301
802-254-8718/
802-251-7203 fax
www.high5adventure.org

SCHOOL NAME   **PROGRAM DATES**

Dear Parent or Guardian,

Welcome to High 5! Please read this document carefully. It contains important information about your child's High 5 activities. If you have any questions please call us.

High 5 Adventure Learning Center (High 5) is a non profit educational organization. High 5 Programs are designed for those in reasonably good health and incorporate a variety of activities, including games and initiatives and more strenuous low and high challenge course elements. The activities may be conducted on the ground or at heights of up to fifty feet, indoors and out. Certain activities may involve close personal contact with other persons. Participants must follow the instructions of the High 5 staff. Each participant may choose the level of his or her participation, recognizing that there is a risk of harm even though minimizing risks is a high priority at High 5. Injuries and other losses can result from, among other causes, moderate to strenuous activity, the possibility of falling, or abrupt contact with other participants, staff, or structures associated with the activity. The outcomes of such risks may include, among others, sprains, breaks, abrasions and other trauma, some of which may be serious. High 5 recommends that participants be covered by health and accident insurance during the time of their participation.

All of High 5's programs are designed to be age appropriate and well within the capabilities of students in reasonably good health. Further, each participant may choose the level of his or her participation.

Managing risks and providing a safe environment is very important in all of our programs at High 5. Please help us by providing the information requested below. Let us know if your child has any condition (current or past) that could affect his/her involvement in all activities and provide any other information relevant to ensuring a safe, enjoyable experience.

If you have any questions about your child's program, don't hesitate to call the High 5 office at 802-254-8718.

STUDENT PROGRAM INFORMATION, ASSUMPTION OF RISKS AND AGREEMENTS OF RELEASE AND INDEMNITY, CONTINUED

....

PART I - GENERAL INFORMATION

STUDENTS NAME   DATE OF BIRTH   SEX: MALE ? FEMALE

ADDRESS

NAME OF INSURANCE CARRIER

NAME OF PARENT/GUARDIAN   HOME PHONE:

ADDRESS   WORK PHONE

In case of emergency and you are not available, please give the name of someone else to notify

NAME   RELATIONSHIP

PHONE   ADDRESS

....

PART II - INSURANCE INFORMATION

Is the student covered by medical insurance?   ◯ Yes   ◯ No

NAME OF INSURANCE CARRIER   POLICY #

NAME OF INSURED   RELATIONSHIP TO STUDENT

PART III-MEDICAL INFORMATION

Does the student have any medical condition (current or past) that could affect his/her ability to fully participate in High 5's programs?   ◯ Yes   ◯ No

If you answered Yes, please explain:

_____

_____

_____

_____

_____

Is the student currently taking any medications?   ◯ Yes   ◯ No

If yes, please give the name of the medication(s) and describe the condition for which it has been prescribed.

_____

_____

_____

_____

Does the student have allergies?   ◯ Yes   ◯ No

Does the student have a history of seizures?   ◯ Yes   ◯ No

Does the student have a chronic or recurring illness?   ◯ Yes   ◯ No

Has the student had a recent injury or infectious disease?   ◯ Yes   ◯ No

If you answered Yes to any part of this question, please explain:

_____

_____

_____

_____

_____

PART IV-ASSUMPTION OF RISKS, AND AGREEMENTS OF RELEASE AND INDEMNITY

In consideration of the services of High 5 in offering these activities, I , for myself and on behalf of my minor child or ward, agree as follows:

Assumption of Risks: I acknowledge that I understand the activities in which I will be participating, and their risks. I understand that the risks are inherent in the activities-that is, they cannot be eliminated without changing the nature and value of the experience. I voluntarily assume all such risks, inherent and otherwise, and whether or not they are described above.

Release and Indemnity: I hereby release and agree to indemnify (that is, defend and pay any judgments, including costs and attorneys fees) High 5 Adventure Learning Center, Inc., its owners, staff members and Board of Directors ("Released Parties") from any and all claims and liabilities arising from an injury or other loss suffered by me related in whole or part to my enrollment or participation in High 5 activities. These agreements of release and indemnity include claims of negligence, but not claims of recklessness or willful misconduct.

Other: In the event of illness or injury, consent is hereby given to provide emergency medical care, hospitalization or other treatment, which may become necessary. If a suite is filed against High 5 or any other released party it must be filed in the County of Windham State of Vermont. Any such suit will be governed by the laws of the State of Vermont, not including those laws which may apply the laws of another jurisdiction.

_____

SIGNATURE OF PARENT/GUARDIAN   **DATE**

_____

NAME OF WORKSHOP   **DATE OF WORKSHOP**

I hereby grant High 5 permission to use, reproduce, or distribute any photographs, films, videotapes and/or sound recordings of me during my training for use in materials it may create, for marketing or other purposes.

_____

SIGNATURE OF PARENT/GUARDIAN   **DATE**

ACCIDENT/INCIDENT REPORT FORM

130 Austine Drive
Brattleboro, VT 05301
802-254-8718/
802-251-7203 fax
www.high5adventure.org

Documentation of accidents, incidents and illnesses that occur during programming is a proactive risk management policy. Collected data can be used to identify problem areas either on the challenge course or in facilitation and participation practices. The following definitions serve as a guide in filling out this form.

Accident: An accident is a situation that involves an injury or serious illness that results in a day's loss or more from school, work or a High 5 program. Medical attention is received.

Incident: An incident is an occurrence where a participant escaped major injury, but still required minor first aid, usually administered by facilitators or chaperones who were present. Bruises and non life-threatening bee stings are examples of incidents.

GENERAL INFORMATION:

NAME   DATE

ADDRESS

PHONE   EMAIL

PROGRAM INFORMATION:

TYPE OF TRAINING   DATE OF TRAINING

INSTRUCTOR'S NAME

ACCIDENT/INCIDENT TRACKING INFORMATION:

TYPE OF OCCURRENCE (ACCIDENT OR INCIDENT) ?DATE OF ACCIDENT/INCIDENT

LOCATION OF ACCIDENT/INCIDENT

NATURE OF INJURY

Narrative: Describe what happened.

ACCIDENT/INCIDENT
REPORT FORM, CONTINUED

Were you seen by a doctor or in the emergency room of a hospital?　　◯ Yes　◯ No ?

_____

IF YES, NAME OF HOSPITAL　　　　　**NAME OF DOCTOR**

_____

ADDRESS

_____

PHONE

If no, explain the reason why medical attention was not sought. If any first aid was administered, please describe.

_____

_____

Were there any witnesses to the occurrence? If yes, list the name, address and phone number of each.

_____

WITNESS　　　　　　　　　　**ADDRESS**

_____

PHONE

_____

STATUS: (PARTICIPANT IN PROGRAM, CHAPERONE OR OTHER)

_____

WITNESS　　　　　　　　　　**ADDRESS**

_____

PHONE

_____

STATUS: (PARTICIPANT IN PROGRAM, CHAPERONE OR OTHER)

_____

SIGNATURES

I hereby affirm that all of the information set forth in this report is accurate and correct.

_____

PARTICIPANT'S SIGNATURE　　　　　**DATE**

_____

STAFF MEMBER COMPLETING REPORT

_____

STAFF SIGNATURE　　　　　　　**DATE**

"NEAR MISS" REPORT FORM

130 Austine Drive
Brattleboro, VT 05301
802-254-8718/
802-251-7203 fax
www.high5adventure.org

Collecting data on near misses or close calls on the High 5 Challenge Course is an important part of our risk management plan. Please complete this form for any occurrence in your program that could have resulted in an Accident/Incident to a participant or staff member. These near misses are situations where no medical care was necessary but the potential for harm was present. This information will be used to assess possible changes in challenge course equipment and practices/procedures.

INSTRUCTOR'S NAME   **DATE OF TRAINING**

TYPE OF TRAINING   **DATE OF INCIDENT**   **TODAY'S DATE**

LOCATION OF INCIDENT   **NATURE OF POTENTIAL INJURY**

In your own words, explain what happened

What, if anything, in your opinion could have been done to prevent this incident?

Were there any witnesses to the occurrence? If yes, list their name and contact information.

WITNESS   **ADDRESS**   **PHONE:**

WITNESS   **ADDRESS**   **PHONE:**

WITNESS   **ADDRESS**   **PHONE:**

I hereby affirm that all of the information set forth in this report is accurate and correct.

INSTRUCTOR'S SIGNATURE   **DATE:**

ROPE USE LOG

130 Austine Drive
Brattleboro, VT 05301
802-254-8718/
802-251-7203 fax
www.high5adventure.org

Element:

Purchase Date:	Rope Length:	Rope Color:

Manufacturer:

DATE	STAFF	# OF USERS	TOTAL # OF USERS*

*Running total of participants using the rope

ROPE INSPECTIONS

DATE	BY	CONDITION

APPENDIX D:

SKILLS VERIFICATION CHECKLIST

HIGH 5 CHALLENGE COURSE :
SKILLS VERIFICATION CHECKLIST

130 Austine Drive
Brattleboro, VT 05301
802-254-8718/
802-251-7203 fax
www.high5adventure.org

Adventure
Learning Center

PARTICIPANT NAME

THE FOLLOWING RUBRICS DESCRIBE THE OBSERVED SKILL LEVEL:

LEVEL 1:
Emerging skills
The participant
demonstrates
minimal skill in
this area.

LEVEL 2:
Developing skills
The participant has
demonstrated this
skill, but requires
continued coaching
and practice time.

LEVEL 3:
Competent skills
The participant
demonstrates this
skill consistently
with care and
accuracy.

LEVEL 4:
Proficient skills
The participant
demonstrates this
skill confidently
and independently,

KNOTS

Demonstrates the ability to tie:

○ Retraced Figure Eight

○ Bowline on a Bight

○ Butterfly Knot

○ Double Fisherman's Knot

○ Girth Hitch

○ Double Figure Eight/Super Eight

○ Clove Hitch/Killick Hitch

○ Prusik Knot

○ Rope Coil (Alpine Coil or Butterfly Coil)

LOW ELEMENTS

Demonstrates the ability to:

○ Teach and model basic spotting techniques; i.e. proper positioning, communication

○ Assess when spotting is necessary during an activity

○ Determine appropriate spotting technique(s) for a variety of low elements

○ Sequence activities appropriately and have the ability to assess a group's readiness for a particular element

ROPE, HARDWARE AND CLIMBING GEAR

Demonstrates the ability to use the following equipment in accordance with the manufacturer's recommendations:

○ Properly put on, adjust and clip into a commercial harness

○ Properly fit and use a chest harness on a participant

○ Properly fit a climbing helmet

○ Properly attach and orient a carabiner

○ Properly set up and position a ladder

Demonstrates the ability to maintain and assess the following equipment:

○ Inspect and evaluate rope, harnesses, carabiners, belay devices, helmets

○ Understand rope and hardware care, use and storage

HIGH CHALLENGE COURSE OPERATIONS

GEAR SET-UP AND RETRIEVAL

Demonstrates the ability to:

○ Set-up a variety of High Challenge Course elements using a haul rope system

○ Operate self-belay lanyards i.e. climbing in a smooth pattern of clip-ins, clipping at waist height or higher, establishing a comfortable working stance at height, minimizing free fall potential to not exceed 6 feet

○ Recognize and use acceptable clip points for self-belay system

○ Properly set-up belay systems on traversing and non-traversing elements

○ Rescue stranded belay gear on a variety of elements

BELAYED ACTIVITIES

Demonstrates the ability to:

○ Run through appropriate pre-climbing procedures including harness check, belay rope knot check, carabiner check, helmet check)

○ Use and apply verbal pre-climbing commands i.e. On Belay? Belay On. Climbing? Climb away

○ Belay properly with a belay device

○ Belay properly on traversing elements

○ Be properly positioned in relation to the climber throughout a climb

○ Appropriately use back-up belayers

○ Appropriately use anchors when belaying a climber heavier than themselves

○ Properly lower off participants on high elements

○ Set-up and manage Australian Belay system

TWO PERSON CUTAWAY RESCUE

Demonstrates the ability to:

○ Quickly and efficiently organize rescue equipment

○ Properly set up rescue belay system

○ Communicate "on belay" with rescue belayer

○ Smoothly and safely access hanging "victim"

○ Properly attach primary prusik

○ Properly attach back-up system

○ Perform a thorough check of all systems prior to cut

ONE PERSON CUTAWAY RESCUE

Demonstrates the ability to:

○ Quickly and efficiently organize rescue equipment

○ Properly set up rescue belay system

○ Lock off belay system (leg wrap or belay gear lock-offs). Remembers to lock off prior to unclipping of self-belays

○ Smoothly and safely access hanging "victim"

○ Properly attach primary prusik

○ Properly set-up back-up system

○ Perform a thorough check of all systems prior to cut

○ Perform a clean lower to the ground

○ Be able to perform a belay escape

SPECIALTY ELEMENTS

Demonstrates the ability to:

Set-up and manage the Holy Cow Swing including:

◯ Correct clip-in procedures for the participant

◯ Correct clip-in technique for the release system

◯ Proper management of the retrieval rope

◯ Appropriate supervision of the pulling team

◯ Maintenance of a clear corridor for the swinger

◯ Properly bringing the participant to stillness after the swing

Set-up and manage the Pamper Pole/Pamper Plank element including:

◯ The proper use of a Just Rite descender

◯ The proper positioning of the belay set-up prior to a jump

◯ Proper clip-in procedures using a rear clip-in and chest harness

◯ Appropriate jumping procedures for the climber

Set-up and manage Zip line operations including:

◯ Proper zip pulley set-up

◯ Proper belay transfer from access belay to static zip belay

◯ Assessing that the zip corridor is clear

◯ Proper take-off procedures for zip participant

◯ Proper instruction and management of take-down procedures at end of zip

Set-up and manage Climbing Tower Operations

◯ Set-up of tower systems

◯ Managing participants on self-belays on tower platform

◯ Proper set-up and management of rappel station

Bibliography

Association for Challenge Course Technology. *Challenge Course Standards: Sixth Edition*. MI: Association of Challenge Course Technology, 2004.

Ashley, Clifford W. *The Ashley Book of Knots*. New York: Doubleday and Co., 1944.

Cain, James, Cummings, Michelle, and Stanchfield, Jennifer. *A Teachable Moment*. Dubuque, IA: Kendall/Hunt Publishing Co., 2005.

Frank, Laurie S. *The Caring Classroom*. Madison, WI: Goal Consulting, 2001.

Padgett, Allen and Smith, Bruce. *On Rope*. Huntsville, AL: National Speleological Society Publication, 1987.

Rohnke, Karl. *Cowstails and Cobras*. Dubuque, IA: Kendall Hunt Publishing Co., 1989.

Ryan, Bob. *The Guide for Challenge Course Operations*. Beverly, MA: Project Adventure, Inc. Publication, 2005.

The Mountaineers/Seattle. *Mountaineering, The Freedom of the Hills: Fifth Edition*. Seattle: The Mountaineers, 1992.

About the Authors

Jim began his adventure career in 1979 and since then has trained thousands of people in the art of adventure. He is one of the founders of High 5 Adventure Learning Center and currently serves as the director but also continues to lead many of High 5's trainings for both new and seasoned adventure practitioners.

During his years at Project Adventure, Jim served in a variety of roles which included lead trainer for skills-based workshops, a member of the Board of Directors, director of the Project Adventure Vermont office and nces throughout the Northeast and Canada.

Jim presents regularly at AEE, ACCT and AAHPERD conferences, regionally and nationally. He currently serves on the Certification Standards Committee of the Association for Challenge Course Technology. He co-authored *Back Pocket Adventure* with Karl Rohnke and has written numerous articles for various publications in the field. He holds a Masters in Education from Salem State College in Salem, MA

Nicki is a 27-year veteran of adventure education. She is one of the founders of High 5 Adventure Learning Center and continues to facilitate training workshops for both beginner and advanced level practitioners. During her years at High 5 and Project Adventure, her keen eye and thorough approach have been instrumental in developing techniques for assessing the technical skills of practitioners. Her skills as a facilitator and her knowledge of adventure education have helped countless programs develop and thrive.

Whether she is leading a workshop, designing adventure curricula for schools and community groups, or facilitating team-building workshops, her passion is in helping adventure practitioners develop programs that are rich in spirit, practical in application and technically up to quality standards. She holds a Masters in Education from the University of Massachusetts in Amherst, MA.

High 5 Adventure Learning Center
130 Austine Drive
Suite 170
Brattleboro, VT 05301

www.high5adventure.org

Important: The practices, procedures and forms presented in this publication are intended to be used, if at all, as guidelines and examples only. Programs vary greatly, including with respect to goals, clients, staff, environments and activities. A program which uses any part of the material furnished in this publication does so at its own risk. Neither High 5 nor any of its staff, directors or owners is responsible for any outcome of such use.

INDEX